WORLD ELITE FORCES

Eric MICHELETTI
Illustrated by Louis MURTIN
Translated by Jean-Pierre VILLAUME

HISTOIRE & COLLECTIONS

ISBN: **2 908 182 25 4**
HISTOIRE & COLLECTIONS
P.O. Box 327, Poole, Dorset BH15 2 RG, UK

CONTENTS

EUROPE

FORMER WARSAW PACT

MIDDLE EAST

ASIA AND AUSTRALASIA

NORTH AND SOUTH AMERICA

AFRICA

4

EUROPE

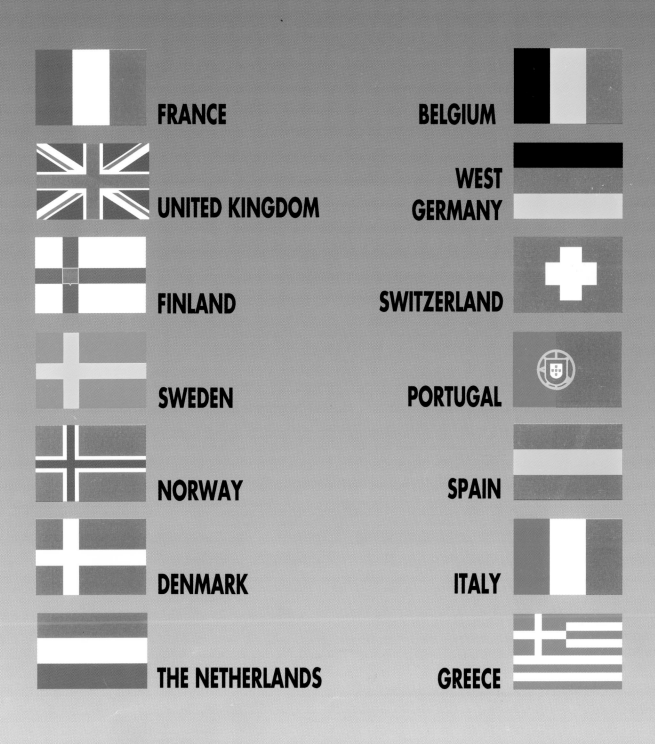

FRANCE

UNITED KINGDOM

FINLAND

SWEDEN

NORWAY

DENMARK

THE NETHERLANDS

BELGIUM

WEST GERMANY

SWITZERLAND

PORTUGAL

SPAIN

ITALY

GREECE

FRENCH PARA LEGIONNAIRE

The decision, in spring 1948, to raise two battalions of Foreign Legion paratroopers was prompted by the French government's requirement for enlarged airborne forces in Indochina. Soon, Legionnaires of 2^e, 3^e REI and 13^e DBLE were gathered into the 3^e REI's airborne company and immediately dispatched into combat. In July of that year, 1er BEP (Bataillon Etranger de Parachutistes) was raised in Algeria and sailed into Haiphong in November. Largely formed from personnel of Legion units in Morocco, 2^e BEP landed at Saigon on 8 February 1949.

On 16 November 1949, the 3^e BEP was raised from members of the 1er REI and based at Setif, Algeria. This was a training and transit unit providing replacements for the two battalions in Indochina. From 1949 to 1955, the Para-Legionnaires were always in the thick of the action and fought on until Dien Bien Phu where many courageous encounters were recorded.

2^e REP was raised in December 1955 from 2^e and 3^e BEP. Quartered in Algeria, it was soon joined by 1er REP which, in September 1955, had inherited the traditions of 1er BEP. Both regiments were heavily involved in combat, serving in open country and in cities. 1er REP was disbanded as punishment for its part in the April 1961 failed putsch against President Charles de Gaulle.

In June 1967, 2^e REP took up quarters in Calvi, Corsica, and in the 1970s, provided companies to the deployment in Chad while, along with other Legion and French Army regular units, the Legionnaires helped maintain the French presence in Djibouti.

On 18 May 1978, 2^e REP was ordered to intervene in Zaire and was dropped over Kolwezi to stem the advance of Katanga rebels and liberate the population. The operation was a complete success.

In September 1982, 2^e REP CCS (command and services company) was sent to Beirut as a peacekeeping force. Again, the Legion proved up to its task. In 1991, one of their companies was dispatched to Rwanda when fighting broke out and since 1992, Legionnaires have contributed forces to the UN peace-keeping deployments in the ex-Yugoslavia and Somalia.

Totalling 1,300 officers and men, 2^e REP is organised into six companies - four specialised combat, one command and services and one recce and support (the latter includes a platoon of Commando de Renseignement et d'Action dans la Profondeur or deep recce free-faller commandos).

Currently, this prestigious unit is the most combat ready of all French Army units. In a matter of hours, it can be put on a war footing and dispatched anywhere in the world to defend French interests. ◻

1982: a grenadier-voltigeur (rifleman) of 2e REP's Command and Services Company during Operation 'Epaulard' in Beirut. The man's F-1 combat fatigues are on standard issue to all French forces, as is the 5.56mm Famas assault rifle. In addition, the Legionnaire carries his PP 6 transceiver over the new model 1978 webbing. Legionnaires in Beirut were issued with large olive drab armbands sporting the French tricolour.

Five REP badges pinned on a green beret and displayed around the standard French airborne forces badge. Top: the regimental badge and from left to right, the four specialised companies' badges: 1st Coy (anti-tank, night and urban warfare); 2nd Coy (mountain); 3rd Coy (amphibious assault) and 4th Coy (sabotage and sniping).

9

PARA 'MÉTRO'

'Pachold!', shouted the Russian pilot. At his command, Capitaine Fred Geille jumped into the void. Geille was one of three French officers sent to the USSR in April 1935 to obtain their jumpmaster ratings and study the development of Soviet airborne forces.

Their report proved a determining factor in the creation of a parachute school at Avignon-Pujaut in southern France and, on 26 November, Geille made the first jump ever in the history of the French airborne forces.

On 2 October 1936, a ministerial decree defining the creation of 601e and 602e Groupements d'Infanterie de l'Air (air force infantry groups) was passed. Placed under French Air Force control, each group comprised a para company and a transport aircraft squadron. Volunteers hailed from all the services and their first group jump took place in May 1937. When the Avignon-Pujaut parachute school folded one year later, more than 150 instructors with more than 2,000 jumps had been trained.

The airborne groups were posted to Africa when the war broke out and hurriedly ferried back to France. 601e was ready to be dropped over the Netherlands when the operation was cancelled. Until their disbandment in July 1940, the two groups operated independently as 'Corps Francs' (shock troops).

In November 1942, the Americans landed in North Africa and took over the 250 paras of 601e who had continued training there unbeknownst to the Germans.

In January 1943, the Fez-trained unit reverted to French Army control and its 1,850 men were commissioned with 1er RCP (Régiment de Chasseurs Parachutistes or airborne regiment). Attached to the 1st French Army, the paras fought in the Vosges mountains, Alsace and on the Rhine. Also raised in North Africa around that time were two other famous assault units: the Bataillon de Choc (shock battalion) that distinguished itself in Corsica, Elba and Provence, and the Groupe des Commandos de France (French Commando Group).

Led by Capitaine Bergé since June 1941, the 1ere Compagnie d'Infanterie de l'Air (airborne infantry company) was transferred to Egypt (minus a unit attached to BCRA, the Free French secret services) and commissioned with the SAS as a French Squadron. Meanwhile, 2e and 3e RCP were trained in Britain and deployed in France and the Netherlands during the 1944-45 campaign. Both units were amalgamated into 2e RCP in August.

From 1946, three types of airborne unit could be distinguished: metropolitan, colonial and Foreign Legion. The 'paras métro' were regulars in RCPs and Bataillons de Choc, whereas the 'paras colo' were volunteer regulars for overseas service and later redesignated as BPCs (Bataillons de Parachutistes Coloniaux or overseas service airborne battalion). The Foreign Legion fielded two BEPs (Bataillon Etranger de Parachutistes or Foreign Airborne Battalion).

A training school was activated in Pau in April 1946 when more paras were needed for Indochina and, although trained for European theatres, several 'métro' units were deployed overseas. From 1946 to 1954, the number of paras fighting in Asia soared from 300 to 25,000, (including locally raised units). The Indochina War was hardly over when another conflict flared up in Algeria.

On 1 March 1951, the 25e Division Aéroportée (25th Airborne Division) was raised, followed in June by another two regiments, 9th and 14th RCP. During the Algerian conflict, the paras reached a high level of proficiency, making few actual combat jumps but pioneering the large-scale tactical use of helicopter insertion. This savage urban and wilderness counter-guerilla war was waged by both sides with the same ruthlessness but eventually won by the paras.

In November 1956, 1er and 2e BCP with units of 11e Choc jumped over Port Said during the Suez Crisis.

When President de Gaulle agreed to Algerian independence in 1961, disgruntled paratroopers of 1er REP and 14e and 18e RCPs spearheaded a short-lived and almost bloodless putsch led by four retired generals. Disbanded after the failed coup, the dissident units were incorporated into the 11e Division Légère d'Intervention (11th Light Airborne Intervention Division) which changed its name several times until 1971 when it became known as 11e DP (division parachutiste or airborne division). In August 1983, 11e DP was integrated with France's Rapid Intervention Force. ☐

A 'brigadier' (corporal) of 1er Escadron of 1er RHP (Régiment de Hussards Parachutistes, airborne light armoured regiment) seen in 1986 on the Tarbes training ground. A sniper assigned to the protection of the company's captain, the man wears F-1 combat fatigues with 1974 Model webbing. He is armed with a scope-fitted 7.62mm FR-F1sniper rifle. The newly introduced F-1helmet and a three-grenade pouch are suspended from his belt. Since 1978 1er RHP has been on duty in all overseas theatres, from Lebanon to Chad.

Top. Airborne qualification badge awarded after 6 automatic jumps. Left: the free-fall badge awarded to paras completing the high altitude operational jump course; right: jumpmaster badge. Bottom: badge awarded to all para units since 1946 and restricted since 1958 to 'métro' and Foreign Legion paras.

FRENCH 'PARA COLO'

The complex lineage and history of French 'paras coloniaux' (Overseas Service Airborne Forces) can be traced back to the creation of the Demi-Brigade de Parachutistes SAS in 1946. The SAS was sent to Indochina when the Vietminh attempted to wrench this colony from French control and the Demi-Brigade became successively known as the Overseas Airborne SAS Half Brigade before being converted in 1948 into the 2e BCCP (Bataillon Colonial de Commandos Parachutistes).

After 2e BCCP further battalions were raised, trained (mainly in Brittany) and dispatched to Indochina in the following order: 2e, 5e, 1e, 6e, 8e and 7e. The Groupement des Parachutistes Coloniaux (Overseas Airborne Commando Group) came into being in 1947 and was based in Brazzaville and Madagascar. One year later, 4e BCCP was raised in Dakar.

In 1951 the BCCPs became BPCs - Bataillons de Parachutistes Coloniaux (Overseas Airborne Battalion) while other units were raised to protect French territories in Africa.

2e BCCP was deployed in Indochina in 1949 and fought successfully in Cochin China and Annam. In February, 3e and 5e BCCP were dropped under fire in the Lao-Kay region to stem the Vietminh offensive. In May 1950, the paras of 3e BCCP intervened successfully at Dong Khé.

After the disaster of the RC 4 (Route Coloniale or Colonial Highway N°4), suffered by the French forces when High Command decided to abandon an indefensible line of posts along RC 4 in north Tonkin, Commander-in-Chief General Jean de Lattre de Tassignies inflicted on the 'Viets' a severe setback at the battle of Day in May 1951. The paras of 7e BCP (strengthened by 2e BEP) played a major part in the victory. At that time, 'colonial' airborne troops included 1e, 2e, 3e, 6e and 7e BPC. The 'paras colos' fought at Nghia Lo in October 1951, Hoa Binh and were involved in a severe combat at Na San where 3e, 5e and 6e BPC killed more than 7,000 Vietminh. When Dien Bien Phu fell to the Vietminh in 1954, most 'colonial para' units had practically been wiped out and had to be recreated from scratch.

The paras left Indochina only to be sent to Algeria one year later with their battalions now expanded into regiments which were then integrated with General Massu's 10th DP (Division Parachutiste or airborne division). 3e RCP was based at Sidi-Ferruch, 2e RPC at Kolea and 6e RPC in Morocco where it remained until 1957 (8e RPC answered to 25e DP). In November 1956, during the Franco-British intervention in Suez, 2e RPC led by Colonel Château-Jobert jumped over Port Said. From 1957 to 1962 'para colo' units were successfully involved in all the major operations against Algerian 'fellagahs', eventually breaking the back of the rebellion.

In 1958, the colonial para regiments became RPIMa (Regiments de Parachutistes d'Infanterie de Marine or airborne marine infantry). In May 1961, the 'para colo' units were gathered within the 11e Division Légère d'Intervention (light intervention division) which became 11e DP in 1971. The Division was subdivided into the 1st Brigade, comprising 3e and 8e RPIMa, and the 2nd Brigade with 2e and 6e RPIMa. These brigades have now been disbanded and 11e DP includes 1e RPIMa (based in Bayonne), 3e RPIMa (Carcassone), 6e RPIMa (Mont-de-Marsan) and 8e RPIMa (Castres). A cadre unit, La Réunion-based 2e RPIMa only comprises one company.

Living up to their lofty traditions, the Overseas Airborne Forces have been involved in all exterior theatres, from Asia to Africa and throughout the Middle East. ❐

Some of the 'para colos' most representative badges and insignia. From left to right and from top to bottom: 1962-74 airborne marine infantry cap badge; airborne cap badge issued from 1958-62 and reintroduced in 1974; 1e Bataillon de Parachutistes Coloniaux badge, Brigade de Parachutistes Coloniaux cloth insignia; Compagnie de Parachutistes d'Infanterie de Marine badge (based in Africa from 1963-75); 6e RPIMa badge; 2e RPC badge (2e RPIMa since 1958); 3e RPC badge (3e RPIMa since 1958).

August 1983: a Corporal of 3e RPIMa in Abéché, Chad, during Operation 'Manta' still wearing the Model 47/56 camouflage fatigues introduced during the Algerian War. Armed with a 5.56mm Famas assault rifle, the 'para colo' is equipped with Model 1974 webbing and magazine pouches. One year later, all units involved in 'Manta' were issued with desert tan shirts and khaki shorts.

13

FRENCH AIRBORNE GENDARME

Created on 1 January 1984 by a ministerial decree, France's EPIGN (Escadron Parachutiste d'Intervention de la Gendarmerie Nationale or Gendarmerie Airborne Intervention Squadron) originated from the EPGM (Escadron Parachutiste de Gendarmerie Mobile or Mobile Gendarmerie Airborne Squadron) that came into being on 1 January 1971 in Mont-de-Marsan. Later, the EPGM was transformed into the 9/11th Airborne Squadron of the Gendarmerie Nationale.

Thanks to their airborne qualification, EPGM members are particulary well suited to handle exceptional situations such as maintaining order, rescue operations or salvage missions. Among others, EPGM contributed a military police unit to the 11e Division Parachutiste (airborne unit) and provided numerous detachments to overseas forces. In 1978, EPGM Gendarmes were sent to Chad (from March 1978 to May 1980) and to Bangui in Central Africa. In 1978, the Squadron contributed forces to the international deployment in Beirut, Lebanon. The missions of the units changed after the Central Administration of the Gendarmerie decided to form the Groupe d'Intervention de la Gendarmerie Nationale IV (Gendarmerie Nationale Intervention Group IV). In 1975, this unit intervened successfully in Corsica against FLNC separatists prior to being disbanded in 1976.

From then on, EPIGN took part in other missions in Corsica and operated alongside the newly-recreated GIGN (which had evolved from the original cadre of GIGN IV) and was involved in a hostage seizure at the Hotel Fech in Ajaccio. The unit intervened again in 1980 when the Plogoff nuclear plant was threatened by demonstrators and in 1981, was deployed yet again near Golfech for the same type of assignment. On 1 January 1984, the unit became known as EPIGN and took up quarters in Satory. In 1984, one of the squadron's platoons was sent to Cyprus following the hijacking of an Air France airliner but was held in reserve with its heavy equipment.

In 1985, EPIGN platoons operated on a rotation basis in Basque country and lent their support to local police brigades in their struggle against terrorism. EPIGN was then sent to New Caledonia when separatists caused troubles in this overseas territory where EPIGN Gendarmes were mostly involved in deep recce and intelligence missions. Around that time other members of EPIGN were sent to the Bois d'Arcy jail to bring rebellious prisoners to heel. In 1986, EPIGN under command of GIGN, took part in a large sweep against criminals in Aix-en-Provence. During the Pope's visit, the squadron was mobilised to provide discreete security.

In 1987, a platoon was sent to Basque country where it collaborated with other Gendarmerie units in their search for ETA terrorists. In July, EPIGN intervened alongside the GIGN to quell riots at the Fleury-Mérogis prison near Paris. From then on, platoons were dispatched to New Caledonia to help maintain order.

From 1988, an EPIGN platoon was permanently based on New Caledonian territory. Supported by an intervention unit, this platoon intervened when French Special Forces attempted to liberate hostages detained by Kanak separatists in caves on Ouvea island. Two units are attached to ground forces units and take part regularly in overseas assignments.

Along with the GSPR (Groupe de Sécurité du Président de la République - President of the Republic's bodyguards) EPIGN answers to GIGS (Groupe de Sécurité et d'Intervention de La Gendarmerie Nationale or Gendarmerie Security and Intervention Group). Ever since its creation in 1984, the unit has been based in Satory, in central France.

The force is subdivided into four platoons of 30-35 men each and complemented by an outside free-faller platoon. Since 1986, one of the four platoons specialises in VIP close protection. Commanded by a Captain, EPIGN comprises five officers and 135 NCOs. Recruiting is done exclusively among volunteers NCOs, applying from within the Departmental and Mobile Gendarmerie. Applicants undergo the same pre-selection tests as airborne forces (psychological and fitness). Run on a twice-yearly basis, each intake numbers about 10 candidates.

The EPIGN Gendarmes are trained to work alongside GIGN and fulfil the same types of mission, which gives an idea of the very high standard of this elite force. ⌐

Above. **A Warrant Officer of EPIGN, Second Platoon, pictured in 1990 at the Camp de Montdésir, Ile de France. EPIGN members are the only Gendarmes issued with the dark blue beret adorned with the Squadron's badge. In keeping with the types of mission with which they are entrusted, EPIGN Gendarmes are kitted out like Special Forces soldiers: their assault vests have built-in magazine pouches with an assault bag and a holster for the regulation handgun. Unlike GIGN members who are armed with HK MP-5s or other submachine-guns of the H & K range, EPIGN Gendarmes are equipped with Famas or FR-F2 sniper rifles.**

From top to bottom: **EPIGN beret badge (introduced in 1978); plastic version of the EPIGN shoulder badge (worn since 1978 and officially confirmed in 1981).**

15

FRENCH MARINE

In 1622 Cardinal de Richelieu (Prime Minister to French King Louis XIII), created the Compagnies Ordinaires de la Mer (Seaborne Infantry Companies) when troops were needed for overseas service. Four years later, this corps was supplemented by a new regiment known as Régiment de la Marine (Marine Regiment). In 1689, the Troupes de la Marine were reorganised into 80 Compagnies Franches d'Infanterie tasked with defending harbours or garrisoning the colonies. This structure was retained until 1762 when the Compagnies were disbanded and replaced by 23 Régiments de la Marine.

By a Royal Decree promulgated on 14 May 1831, a further two regiments were raised to garrison French colonies. In 1838, another regiment was formed and the three units were respectively known as 1st, 2nd and 3rd Régiments d'Infanterie de Marine.

Throughout the 19th Century, these regiments were actively involved in wars and played a major part during the colonial expansion. The 'Marsouins' (porpoises) fought in Mexico, Madagascar, Indochina and Western Africa. In 1899, there were 18 such regiments. The French colonial empire was then at its zenith, and much of the territories had been secured with the Troupes de Marine's participation.

On 1 January 1901, the Troupes de Marine were redesignated Troupes Coloniales (Colonial Troops) and comprised some 20 colonial infantry regiments (1st to 18th Régiment d'Infanterie Coloniale, with 21st and 22nd RIC), three regiments of Senegalese Rifles (1st, 2nd and 3rd Régiments de Tirailleurs Sénégalais), two regiments of Madagascan rifles (1st and 2nd Régiments de Tirailleurs Malgaches), three regiments and three independent colonial artillery groups.

The number of units was increased during the Great war and brought to 28 infantry regiments and 23 artillery regiments. They fought on all fronts, from the Marne in France to the Balkans. When World War Two broke out in 1940, the Troupes de Marine took part in the battle of France, then fought on in North Africa until 1941. Later, they were integrated with the 9th Division d'Infanterie Coloniale and were in action until Germany collapsed in 1945. The Indochina campaign followed. To comply with NATO's requirements, France had to supplement its 'colonial infantry' with armoured, airborne, signals and engineer units.

On 1 December 1958, the colonial troops reverted back to their former designation as Régiment d'Infanterie de Marine. In the 60s, new measures modified the establishment of the Troupes de Marine with numerous services being transferred to the ground forces. In December 1967, their overseas role was clearly defined, with these troops being able to intervene at short notice with all available means (advanced or airborne forces).

Currently, the French Army's 9th Division d'Infanterie de Marine (9e DIMA) numbers 8,000 men distributed among 7 regiments. The division contributes one motorised infantry division to the Rapid Intervention Force (Force d'Action Rapide). With its headquarters in Nantes, it comprises 9e RCS, 1e RIMa, 2e RIMa, 3e RIMa, RICM, 11e RAMa, and 48e RI. Both 4e and 21e RIMa are integrated with 6e DLB 6th Light Armoured Division). Advanced intervention forces include 5e RIAOM in Djibouti, 33e RIMA in Martinique, 41e BIMa on Guadelupe Island, 9e BIMa in Guyana, 6e BIMa in Gabon, 23e BIMa in Senegal and 43e BIMa in Ivory Coast.

9e DIMa elements have been involved in Tchad (Operations Tacaud in 1978-79, Manta in 1983-84 and Epervier in 1986), in Beyruth (1982-84) and Kuwait (1990-91). During Operation Daguet, codename for France's intervention in the Gulf war, Troupes de Marine contributed one third of the whole French deployment. Troupes de Marine regiments are large units numbering 1,300 to 1,400 men, most of them career soldiers. Their modern equipment enables them to be deployed quickly and efficiently in case of crisis.

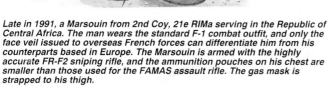

Late in 1991, a Marsouin from 2nd Coy, 21e RIMa serving in the Republic of Central Africa. The man wears the standard F-1 combat outfit, and only the face veil issued to overseas French forces can differentiate him from his counterparts based in Europe. The Marsouin is armed with the highly accurate FR-F2 sniping rifle, and the ammunition pouches on his chest are smaller than those used for the FAMAS assault rifle. The gas mask is strapped to his thigh.

Right: Various Troupes de Marine badges: From top to bottom and from left to right: 1e RIMa, 2e RIMa, Troupes de Marines metal beret badge, 3e RIMa, 4e RIMa, 21e RIMa and RICM. Lack of space prevents us from presenting the RIAOM and BIMa badges. (Doursoux collection).

French marine-commandos during a combined-arms
exercise in Senegal. The men belong to the
Commando de Penfetenyo.

FRENCH MARINE COMMANDO

The French marine Commandos are heirs to the famous 4th Franco-British Commando set up in 1942 in the Scottish Highlands and notorious for their strong *'esprit de corps'*. Composed mostly of Free French, this unit distinguished itself during the winter of 1943-44 on the cliffs of the Pays de Caux, and won fame on 6 June 1944 in Ouistreham where, led by Lt-Cdr Kieffer, 177 commandos breached German lines. In spite of crippling losses, there was no flinching from the men who wore the green beret cocked sideways in British fashion.

The Marine Commandos were later involved in the massive operation against the Walcheren island in Holland where 500 Marine Commandos defeated 1,500 enemies. In the closing stages of the war, the Green Berets served on the North Sea coast from where they carried out numerous raids against German positions.

In 1946, the French Navy created a training centre at Sirocco, near Algiers, with officers and soldiers from the former Kieffer Commando. From July 1945 to December 1947, six commando units were created and given the names of officers killed in action. Commandos Treppel, François, De Montfort, Jaubert, Hubert and de Penfentenyo came into being and were soon dispatched to Indochina where they operated mainly along the Annam coast, in the Mekong Delta and in Tonkin. In one famous episode, Commando François lost more than 50% of its members in a desperate stand near the Nim-Binh church.

In 1953, the Hubert commando became a combat diver unit while Commandos Treppel, De Penfentenyo left Indochina for Algeria where they were grouped into the Marine Demi-Brigade. In late 1956, Commandos Hubert, de Penfentenyo, Jaubert and Treppel - Commando François had become a reserve unit in the meantime - took part in the Suez operation and from 1957 to 1962 were involved in numerous actions in Algeria.

The GROUFUMACO (GROUpement des FUsiliers MArins COmmandos) was briefly based at Toulon prior to being transferred to Lorient (with the exception of the Commando Hubert combat divers who remained in Saint Mandrier).

Since 1976, the French Navy has maintained a commando in the Indian Ocean on six-month tours. From September 1983 to March 1984, Commando De Montfort and Commando Treppel were deployed alternativaly in Beirut as part of the Didon IV mission and deployed alongside the international force in Lebanon.

GROUFUMACO is the ground component of the French Navy and is trained to carry out airborne and seaborne missions such as the coastal amphibious recce or securing beachheads before a landing. In peacetime, the commandos are primarily tasked with maritime police duties (shipping control).

GROUFUMACO's ranks include numerous specialists: combat divers, free-fallers, swimmers, canoeists and sharpshooters. All the commandos are parachute-qualified and trained in heliborne transport. They can be included in any airmobile deployment. The Green Berets are issued with the latest in armament: FAMAS assault rifles, HK MP-5As and SD submachine-guns, FRF-1 and FRF-2 sniping rifles. For anti-tank warfare, the commandos use 90mm LRACs and Milans.

GROUFUMACO's current establishment amounts to 579 officers, NCOs and rank and file.   ❒

A leading seaman from the «Commando de Penfentenyo», during the 1992 exercise «N' Jambour VI», in Senegal. Still equiped with the TR PP 13 set, this radio-operator is wearing his green beret, according to the British fashion. His field dress, webbing and FAMAS riffle is standart. He is also wearing a camo cheche-scarf, very popular for overseas operations.

Right:
Displayed around the 'Marine Commando' cap badge (designed in February 1944): from left to right and from top to bottom, the insigna of Commandos De Montfort, François, De Penfentenyo, Treppel and Jaubert .

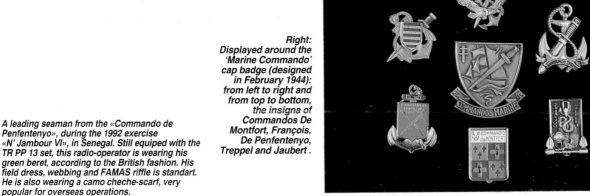

Marsouins of RIAOM rush towards an enemy strongpoint while Sagaie light tanks provide fire support.

Full alert on Orange-Caritat air base! An intruder has just been reported in the compound. Leaping out of the VIB (the air force version of the VAB APC), Air Force Commandos are about to return fire, supported by the VIB's 20mm gun.

FRENCH AIR FORCE COMMANDO

Like the early French airborne forces from which it is descended, GFCA (Groupement des Fusiliers Commandos de l'Air or Air Force Comando Group) answers to French Air Force command. Headquartered at Nîmes-Courbessac Air Base, this airborne force is tasked with defending and reinforcing air force bases, as well as testing equipment, training and assessing ground defenses.

On 12 March 1966, the French Air Force (Armée de l'Air) set up GCPA 541 (Groupement des Commandos Parachutistes de l'Air or Air Force Airborne Commando Group 541), and this unit fought throughout the Algerian War. Organised into five commandos, GCPA was involved in air base security duties and took part in search-and-destroy missions against FLN Algerian dissidents. As a reward for its performance, GCPA received its own flag in February 1959 and operated as an independent unit since until it was disbanded in 1961. However, Bremgarten-based CCPA (Compagnie des Commandos Parachutistes de l'Air or Air Force Airborne Commando Company) was retained and soon converted into a security squadron.

That same year, EFCA (Escadron des Fusiliers Commandos de l'Air or Air Force Commando Squadron) was created in Nîmes to train personnel specialising in the defence of air force bases. EFCA was then known as EFCI (Escadron des Fusiliers Commandos d'Intervention or Intervention Commando Squadron), but its denomination changed in 1976 when the unit adopted its present name of GFCA. Since 1979, GFCA has had its own headquarters, answering to Air Force command and is tasked with security missions as defined by the French Air Force.

Commanded by a general, GFCA numbers about 60 sub-units known as Escadrons de Protection et d'Intervention (Protection and Intervention Squadrons), as well as GIICA (Groupement d'Instruction et d'Intervention des Commandos de l'Air or Air Intervention Commando Training Group). The largest unit of GFCA, GIICA is based in Nîmes and is responsible for training commando and dog handling personnel. Currently, some 7,000 men (5,000 of whom are conscripts) serve in the ranks of GFCA and are colloquially known as 'Fuscos'. Air commandos also train in 'CFIC' centers at Drachenbronn, Evreux and Saintes.

Recruits undergo six-month basic training before commissioning with active units, while cadets receive a further four-weeks tuition. In each intake, 40 volunteers receive specific training prior to induction into the Nîmes security and intervention squadron, GFCA's only paratroop unit.

In the 1980s, Air Force Commandos have been deployed in Africa, the Middle East (during Operations 'Manta' and 'Epervier') and also took part in Operation 'Daguet' against Iraq. In seems likely that, in the near future, the contribution of Air Force Commando to overseas deployments will become increasingly heavy.

NCO belonging to a Protection and Intervention Squadron pictured in Nîmes-Courbessac in 1992. The man is clad in the standard French Air Force issue olive green outfit and wears the dark blue beret with 'Fusco' metal badge. He is equipped with an F-1 helmet and a FAMAS assault rifle fitted with an OB-50 night scope. The heavy cargo bag worn under the ventral parachute is particularly noteworthy.

French Air Commando badges: Top: standard metal badge (worn on the beret). Left: 42/103 Air Base Protection Squadron badge; 42/103 Air Base Protection Squadron cloth insignia; Nîmes EPI 1/301 Air Commando NCO school cloth insignia.This unit has retained the title and traditions of former 602 GIA. The eagle is identical to the GFCA's badge and sports the motto Sicut aquila (like an eagle).

23

BRITISH PARA

Raised by Sir Winston Churchill in 1940, the Parachute Regiment has been involved in more than 50 campaigns since the end of World War 2 and ranks deservedly among Britain's most prestigious units

Numbering 370 men, the first British airborne unit was made up of personnel from 2 Commando. However, its ranks swelled quickly with volunteers, and the paras of 2nd Airborne Brigade created in July 1942, were ferried to Tunisia and soon became known as *'die roten Teufel'* (the red devils) by the Germans.

In 1943, the Brigade jumped over Sicily; they later became 1st Airborne Division. Meanwhile, 6th Airborne Division was being formed back in Britain to spearhead the British forces during the June 1944 Normandy landings. In August, 2nd Independent Brigade (levied from the 1st Division) was dropped over Provence to cut German communication lines. At the end of September, the paras of 1st Division jumped with the Polish Brigade into the Arnhem inferno. The Red Devils further distinguished themselves during Operation 'Varsity' that paved the way for the Rhine crossings.

Although the ranks of British airborne forces were severely trimmed in the years that followed World War 2, men of the Parachute Regiment were still being posted to all territories flying the Union Jack: paras were deployed in Palestine (until 1947), in Malaysia, fought on the Suez Canal at Port Said in 1956, in Cyprus (1964), Aden (1965) and Borneo. From 1969 to 1972, they were controversially involved in internal security missions in Northern Ireland. During the 1982 Falklands War they came into the limelight again when two battalions of the Parachute Regiment demonstrated that British paras could emulate their predecessors of Tunisia and Arnhem fame.

Britain's airborne forces are issued with the same armament as other infantry units: 5.56mm SA-80 assault rifles and ISW support weapons. Accurate on the firing range, these new weapons were found to be rather fragile in practice as they cannot withstand frequent parachuting, forcing soldiers to carry their weapons only when jumping into action. To tackle enemy armour, paras have a heavier allotment of Milan anti-tank missiles than other infantry formations.

There are currently three battalions of the Parachute Regiment in the regular army, (1 Para, 2 Para and 3 Para) and a further two battalions in the territorial army (4 Para and 10 Para). Two of the three regular Parachute Regiment Battalions rotate regularly into 5 Airborne Brigade as the In Role Battalions where they alternate as the LPBG (Leading Parachute Battalion Group) and the FUBPG (Follow Up Parachute Battalion Group). The Brigade now has full parachute-trained organic supporting arms (light artillery, engineers, signals, transport etc). The Brigade fields a company of pathfinders who are trained to land covertly ahead of the main force to prepare the landing sites.

The making of a para requires five months of arduous training, and 'wings' are awarded after eight jumps (including two from a balloon). ❏

1981: a para from 3 Battalion takes a cigarette break during a patrol in South Armagh. The private wears the Model 1978 DPM parachute smock with matching cotton trousers (preferred to synthetic fibre garments which melt and stick to flesh when hit by petrol bombs or tracers). Webbing is '58 Pattern worn with large airborne Bergen rucksack and high leg, privately bought German paratrooper's boots. The beret is adorned with the black badge, and the weapon is a 7.62mm L 72A light machine-gun.

From left to right and from top to bottom: Cadet Corps airborne badge; airborne forces shoulder title, Parachute Regiment metal badge (worn on maroon beret); black cap badge, worn increasingly on combat gear; patches representing the famous Pegasus designed by artist Edward Seago. Centre: the qualification badge awarded after eight jumps, and displayed above the service dress maroon belt fitted with a silver buckle adorned with the Parachute Regiment badge.

ROYAL MARINE

The Royal Marines trace their roots back to 1664 when the Duke of York and Albany's Maritime Regiment of Foot, later renamed Lord High Admiral's Regiment, was raised. For the first time, soldiers were trained to fight on board ship as well as ashore, and for more than three centuries, participated in all wars waged by Britain around the world. In 1805, some 2,700 Royal Marines were embarked on RN ships when Napoleon's fleet was defeated at Trafalgar. They saw action in Sudan (1898), China (1900) and during the Boer War.

Some 55,000 men strong at the end of the Great War, the Royal Marines fought at sea and on land and distinguished themselves in famous actions such as Ostende, Gallipolli and Zeebruge. Totalling 12,000 men at the outbreak of World War 2, the Royal Marines' first intervention took place in Norway where they were sent to protect allied forces. Raised in 1942, the Royal Marine Commando took part in the ill-fated Dieppe operation. In 1943, the force was disbanded and split into several commando units which landed in Italy (September 1943), Walcheren (September 1944), and Antwerp; while 45 Commando was deployed in Burma in January 1945.

In the postwar years, the Royal Marines were engaged in all major British operations and deployed in Palestine, Malaysia, Cyprus, Kuwait, Aden, Tanzania, Borneo and Belize. During the Korean War in 1951, 41 Commando (attached to the US Marines 1st Division) successfully broke out from Chosin, losing 70 men killed out of a force of 200. In 1946, 40, 42 and 45 Commandos of 3rd Brigade spearheaded the landing at Port Said during the Suez Crisis. In the 1960s, the jungles of Borneo gave the Royal Marines the opportunity to distinguish themselves again by helping the Sultanate of Brunei resist Indonesian pressure. In 1964, Marines were dispatched to Aden and for four years, fought rebellious tribes in the Radfan mountains. Since 1971, following Britain's withdrawal from her Middle and Far East possessions, the Marines have been redeployed as an assault force and trained in guarding NATO's northern flank.

In more recent times their amphibious capabilities contributed again in the 1982 Falklands War. In that conflict, 42, 42 and 45 Commandos landed at San Carlos, and from there, 42 and 45 Cdos. stormed the Argentinian positions defending Port Stanley.

Currently, the Royal Marines are organised into two main commands, and total 7,750 men distributed into three-battalion brigades. The force comprises one artillery regiment, two engineer squadrons (independent), one helicopter squadron, one logistics and several special units (the Special Boat Squadron, two recce squadrons and the Comacchio Group raised in 1980 to fight terrorism.)

Their standard weapon is the SA-80 assault rifle, also used in the light machine-gun role in its bipod-mounted LSW variant. ❐

Royal Marines badges and insignia. From left to right and from top to bottom: Royal Marines Light Infantry badge; current cap badge; subdued cap badge; World War 2 all-ranks badge; walking-out dress badge; Number One dress lapel badge; shoulder metal badge; Royal Marines Commando shoulder title, airborne cloth badge awarded to parachute qualified Marines; RM airborne cloth qualification badge.

A Royal Marine Commando during the 1982 Falklands war. Carrying a heavy Bergen the man is clad in the standard DPM combat uniform and issued with the Pattern 58 webbing. Watertight gaiters are worn over high mountain shoes and his hands are protected by 'Northern Ireland' type gloves. Partially wrapped with hessian, his weapon is the well-proved Bren light machine-gun, shown here in its FM L4A4 version rechambered for NATO 7.62 ammunition. In service since World War 2 this weapon was used with deadly effect against the Argentinians. The RM 'globe' badge is worn on the green beret. Field dressings dangle from his belt and an L1A3 smoke grenade is clipped to the webbing.

7TH DEO GURKHA RIFLES

GURKHA

Loyal to the British crown for over 175 years, the Gurkhas live up to the image of soldiers who, like the French Foreign Legionnaires, are ready to lay down their lives for a country which isn't theirs. Depending on one's point of view, the Gurkhas can be regarded as a leftover from the British Empire or as mercenaries committed to the defence of foreign interests. Both Nepal and Britain, however, benefit from this arrangement as it provides thousands of jobs and pensions for young Nepalese while in return, it enables Britain to recruit mettlesome and tough soldiers, famous for their staunch loyalty and ready to be deployed in all theatres.

The relationship between Britain and Nepal dates back to the 19th century when, in 1813 and 1815, the British clashed with the Nepalese on the borders of the huge Indian Empire. The victors were so impressed by the fighting qualities of the Nepalese highlanders that they raised three Gurkha battalions as early as 1815. Since then and for more than a century, the Gurkhas have constituted a sizeable component of the British Indian Army and distinguished themselves in both world wars. Their reputation of obdurate fighters was already well established.

In the Great War, the Gurkhas were deployed against the Turks and fought them in Gallipoli and in Mesopotamia. In World War 2, they were deployed in Italy and later in Burma where they fought on until 1945.

Following the 1947 partition of India, Gurkha troops were shared between the newly-raised Indian Army (1st, 4th, 5th, 8th and 9th Gurkha Rifles) and the British Army (2nd, 6th, 7th and 10th Gurkha Rifles).

Their loyalty unaltered by this reorganisation, British Gurkha units were soon pitted against communist guerillas in Malaysia. This conflict gave the Himalayan soldiers the opportunity to make the most of their redoubtable jungle warfare skills. In 1967, they performed successfully in Borneo against Indonesian troops. When the British left the Malaysian peninsula, the Gurkhas were transferred to Hong Kong and further added to their prestige when, in 1982, they took part in the recapture of the Argentinian-occupied Falklands. The 1st Battalion, 7th Duke of Edinburgh's Own Gurkha Rifles landed at San Carlos Bay along with the 1st Infantry Brigade and participated in the final thrust against Port Stanley.

Gurkhas are still recruited in the Kingdom of Nepal and may enlist at 17 (applicants always outnumber vacancies). Minimum service duration is five years and the compulsory retirement age is 50. Newly inducted recruits train in Hong Kong for nine months prior to commissioning with a Gurkha Battalion. With relatively few British officers serving in their ranks, Gurkha battalions are organised like standard British infantry units and are led by native officers and NCOs who have risen through the ranks.

Headquartered at Hong Kong, Gurkha Field Force comprises 1st and 2nd Battalions King Edwards VII's Own Gurkha Rifles (the Sirmoor Rifles), the 1st Battalion 6th Queen Elizabeth's Own Gurkha Rifles, the 1st Battalion, 7th Duke of Edinburgh's Own Gurkha Rifles and the 1st Battalion, 10th Princess Mary's Own Gurkha Rifles.

In the 1960s, Gurkha battalions were supplemented by ancillary units such as engineers, signals, transport and military police while the airborne and artillery units were disbanded.

The future of these elite soldiers however looks rather clouded as no other posting will be available to them when the British leave Hong Kong in 1997. Furthermore, the language problem combined with the giant strides of military technology make the Gurkhas' prospects even bleaker and are likely to spell their doom before the turn of the century. ❑

Selection of Gurkha units badges (about 60 are known to exist). From top to bottom and from left to right: 8th Gurkha Rifles cap badge (raised in 1824 and disbanded in 1947, this regiment fought with conspicuous gallantry in France during the Great War and in World War 2, distinguishing itself again in Italy and Burma); sleeve 'wings'; Gurkha Engineer Regiment badge (raised in 1948); airborne qualification badge (designed in the 1960s but never issued); 1953-65 Gurkha Transport Regiment badge; Gurkha Staff Band badge.

31

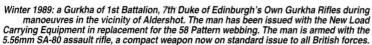

Winter 1989: a Gurkha of 1st Battalion, 7th Duke of Edinburgh's Own Gurkha Rifles during manoeuvres in the vicinity of Aldershot. The man has been issued with the New Load Carrying Equipment in replacement for the 58 Pattern webbing. The man is armed with the 5.56mm SA-80 assault rifle, a compact weapon now on standard issue to all British forces.

SPECIAL BOAT SQUADRON

The Special Boat Squadron is undoubtedly the most famous among the smaller, highly specialised units operating within the Royal Marines - itself an elite force. Trained for seaborne operations and selected from among the best members of the Brigade, SBS are very discreet soldiers whose exploits are often publicized only years after they have been accomplished.

The Squadron originated in World War 2 when special units were needed for raiding and reconnoitring the shores of Europe. This hard-earned experience acquired in wartime is still passed on in spite of the many cutbacks and amalgamations affecting the British forces.

In the war years, the Amphibious School of the Royal Marines (formerly located at Eastney and now at Poole in Dorset) included a 'Small Raids Wing', later redesignated 'the Special Boat Company' and finally 'Special Boat' squadron in 1977. Its major task consisted in amphibious operations, with the emphasis on sabotage, reconnaissance and demolition. The SBS took an active part in World War 2 and is particularly remembered for its daring actions against German installations (in one of their most celebrated raids, SBS commandos paddled up the Gironde estuary in kayaks to lay charges on German ships).

In the post war years, the SBS have seen action in Oman, Borneo and the Falklands. In the latter conflict, they were ashore in South Georgia long before the Task Force arrived, having been flown in from the UK in a C-130 and then parachuted into the sea near a British submarine in the South Atlantic. The submarine took them closer inshore and the commandos completed their journey in inflatable boats. According to rumours, SBS patrols delivered by submarine HMS Onyx operated on the Argentine mainland throughout the campaign. The SBS and SAS were deployed in the Falklands long before the main assault and explored the shore at San Carlos where they silenced an Argentinian outpost overlooking the landing site.

Also on strength with the SBS is a Boat Squadron equipped with kayaks and closed circuit aqualungs for underwater missions. (Unofficially, the SBS are currently responsible for the security of British offshore oil and gas rigs).

SBS personnel are exclusively recruited from Royal Marine Commandos volunteers. All applicants - irrespective of rank - undergo physical and psychological tests followed by a three-week selection procedure. Successful candidates then go on a 15-week training course in seamanship, navigation, demolition, diving and advanced weapons handling. The last phase is devoted to a four-week parachute course following which successful candidates are commissioned with an operational Special Boat Section. The SBS is organised into several sections composed of fully autonomous four-man patrols. SBS officers and Marines do not have to leave the force after a set period but, as often in elite units, are forced to do so to obtain promotion.

Standard armament includes M-16 Armalite rifles, M-203 grenade launchers and a special, sound-suppressed version of the British 9mm L34A 1 Sterling submachine-gun. Boats include paddle boards, specially produced Klepper Mk 13 collapsible boats and the larger Geminis powered by 40hp outboard engines.

The SBS can be regarded as one of the world's best trained units of this type. ◻

Great Britain, 1985. An SBS combat diver in neoprene suit and equipped with a British-made closed circuit aqualung. The bulky breathing bag is noteworthy. In his right hand, the man holds a navigation board (compass and depth gauge) and in the left hand a five-barrelled 5mm H&K P-11 underwater pistol loaded with explosive darts fitted with electronic fuses. A knife is strapped to his right ankle while the explosive charge (not shown in the picture) is fastened to the back for freedom of movements during the underwater approach.

SBS badges and insignia. From top to bottom and from left to right. RM airborne cloth badge; RM tropical suit airborne badge; swimmer-canoeist sleeve badge; swimmer canoeist patch (rank and file). Centre: unofficial SBS badge.

BRITISH SAS

Britain's Special Air Service has always fired the public's imagination ever since it was raised on the banks of the Nile in 1941.

The idea for the Special Air Service originated with Lt-Col Dudley Clarke in 1940 but it was in fact Lt David Sterling who created the SAS one year later while serving with 8 Commando, a unit attached to the 3,000-man 'Layforce' deployed in North Africa from November 1940.

In October 1941, Sterling was authorised to muster 66 men from the 'Layforce' into 'L Detachment', a small commando outfit tasked with attacking the overstretched German supply lines in the Western Desert. Tragically, the first mission of 'L Detachment' on 16 October 1941 against German airfields was a dismal failure after desert winds completely disrupted the jump. According to the plan, 62 officers and men were to be dropped near German airfields and ferried back to safety by the Long Range Desert Group after destroying the aircraft. In the event, only 22 officers and men, including Sterling, made it back to the Allied lines.

This setback notwithstanding, 'L Detachment' was expanded into a 390-man force and became 1st Special Air Service Regiment (or 1 SAS). The force soon included a Free French and a Greek squadron. After several reshuffles, an SAS Brigade was formed in Scotland in January 1944. It comprised two British (1 and 2 SAS) and two French (3 and 4 SAS) regiments, one Belgian squadron (later designated 5 SAS) and one signals squadron. In addition to the numerous raids they carried out in North Africa, the SAS also fought in Italy, France, Belgium, Holland and Germany. Always operating behind enemy lines and facing overwhelming odds, SAS action often proved decisive.

At the end of the war, British Command hastily divested itself of 'private armies' and 5 SAS was handed over to the Belgians while in October 1945, 3 and 4 SAS were integrated with French forces. British military experts, however, were only too aware of the vital role SAS-type units could play in a future conflict and the famous 'Artists' Rifles' (a territorial unit) was soon converted into 21 SAS (Artists) - (Volunteers). When an 'Emergency' flared up in the then British protectorate of Malaysia, General Michael Calvert, former commander of the SAS Brigade, took the matter in his own hands and formed the Malaysian Scouts Special Air Service Regiment (renamed 22 SAS soon afterwards).

In 1958, the SAS was dispatched to Oman to quell a a rebellion. Then it was sent Borneo in January 1963 just as another war broke out in Aden. Referred to as the 'happy time' by the SAS, this period saw the three squadrons of 22 SAS involved in ceaseless rotations between the conflicts in Borneo and Aden.

In 1969, the 'troubles' began in Northern Ireland and the SAS found itself involved in a 'dirty war' against the IRA - one which has continued unabated to the present day. Around that time, other troubles flared up in Oman. In July 1972, during the fight at Mirbat, a party of SAS numbering less than 10 men proved more than a match for some 250 insurgents. The SAS lent its expertise in special operations - like the hostage and rescue missions at Mogadishu in 1977 and, in the same year, operated alongside Germany's GSG in Holland when a train hijacked by Moluccan terrorists was stormed to free the hostages.

Its most celebrated feat remains the May 1980 assault of the Iranian Embassy in London, an action that put the SAS in the limelight literally on live television, and showed them as an anti-terrorist force without rival. But it was the Falklands War that gave the SAS the opportunity to remind the world that its men ranked among the best soldiers. The SAS troops were the first to land in the islands. On 14 May 1992, on Pebble the SAS destroyed no fewer than 11 Argentinian aircraft in a raid reminiscent of the deadly forays their forerunners of 40 years ago used to conduct against Axis forces.

During the Gulf War, the SAS was deployed in the early stages of Operation 'Grandby' - the code name for UK operations in the Gulf - and operated in small sections behind Iraqi lines. Its most widely publicised action was the location and destruction of Scud missile launchers in Iraqi territory. The task was to locate the launchers, then relay their coordinates to American aircraft (although on some occasions, the SAS destroyed the launchers immediately). The fact that the SAS were operating within their own lines also had a potent psychological effect on the Iraqis' morale.

Today's SAS is composed of three regiments of 600-700 men each, with only 22 being an active unit. (21 and 23 SAS are kept in reserve.) The SAS is backed up by two signals squadrons, one active and one in reserve (63 Sqn). The British SAS are certainly among the most proficient soldiers of all, selected according to stringent criteria and undergoing the toughest training in the world. Close ties exist between the members of regular and territorial units and, all regiments are regularly involved in exercises to ensure that the highest professional standards are maintained and all that the benefits of recent professional experience are passed on. ❑

A British SAS man in the Falklands, May 1982. The SAS troops were among the first to land covertly on the islands and were mainly involved in deep recce and sabotage missions. The man's DPM smock has more pockets than the standard model. He is armed with an XM-77, the shorter version of the M-16 assault rifle, fitted with two 20-round magazines taped together for quick reloading. Four magazine pouches derived from the 58 Pattern model are suspended from his belt.

Main SAS badges. From top to bottom and from left to right: SAS shoulder title, airborne qualification badge (overseas variant); famous SAS badge (nicknamed 'the sabre'), SAS collar metal badges, Number One dress SAS airborne qualification badge; overseas airborne qualification badge. Centre: 1941 SAS cloth insignia worn on the beige beret, flanked by several SAS cap badges.

FINNISH PARA-COMMANDO

In April 1941, Finland established its first jump school in Luonetjarvi and soon afterwards some 14 NCOs were coached in airborne techniques by Major Erho, a parachute enthusiast for over 20 years. Using captured Soviet equipment, several airborne teams were trained and carried out deep forays behind the Soviet lines in the opening stages of Operation 'Barbarossa'.

In 1942, the air force organised a jump course on Ontulla air base and the initial intake of 40 men was trained by an instructor who had graduated in Germany. During the following years, the paras were commissioned with a deep recce unit, the 4th Independant Battalion, and operated inside the Soviet Union until the end of August 1944 when they disappeared amidst the collapse of Axis forces.

In 1961, airborne tuition was entrusted to an officer who had attended several jump schools abroad and who produced such positive results that a parachute school (Laskuvarjojäärkäkoulu or Airborne Jaeger School) was formed shortly afterwards in Utti. Like their Swedish counterparts, Finland's paras were drilled in parachute, scouting, commando and survival techniques.

Selection procedures have hardly changed since the 1960s: would-be paras are selected from among national servicemen or 'regulars', and serve for 11 instead of eight months. Every year, some 200 applicants volunteer but only half of them passes the stringent medical, psychological and physical tests. They then undergo five weeks basic and three weeks jump training. To obtain their 'wings' they must accomplish eight jumps (four individually, two in group, one by night and one over woodland) and are awarded their bronze 'wings' before a jump over water.

The paras spend their full 11 months of active duty at the Airborne Jaeger School where they receive further training in parachuting, Ranger-type action, sabotage, engineering, sniping, mortar and medium-weapon firing. In wartime, they would be assigned to reserve platoons controlled by the 'Lapland' Infantry battalion based at Sodankya in Finland's northernmost tip, or serve with the Konu Infantry Brigade defending the north of the country. Jaeger are also deployed with the Botnie Infantry Brigade based at Oulu in the west, or operate as independent Sissojä, the light infantry ski units which harried the Soviets with telling effects during the 1939-40 war. 'Regulars' are permanently commissioned to platoon-sized units attached to army brigades, and carry out recce and sabotage behind enemy lines. Their missions are identical to those of the Rannikijääkanpataljoona (Coastal Jaeger Battalion).

1989: heir to the famous 'Sissojä' (guerillas) who harrassed the Russians mercilessly during World War 2, a Finnish para of the Kanu Brigade during a winter exercise in Lapland. Kitted out in the camouflage outfit on specific issue to Finnish airborne forces, this volunteer is commissioned with one of the brigade's recce platoons. He is armed with an M-62 7.62mm assault rifle (locally manufactured version of the Soviet AK-47). A drawback of the standard AK bayonet and spare magazines is that they rattle as they dangle from the webbing (of course in combat conditions they would be muffled). The magazine pouches are made of thick canvas.

Representative Finnish insignia and airborne qualification badges. From left to right: 3rd class badge (awarded after eight jumps); cap badge worn on the maroon beret; 2nd class airborne badge. Below. 1st Class airborne badge (awarded for 150 jumps).

SWEDISH RANGER

In the 1950s, a dozen Swedish officers were sent to the United States, Britain and Belgium for parachute training. They later formed the cadre of the Army Parachute-Jaeger School (Armans fallskarmsjägerkola) at Karlsborg. The first course took place in February 1952.

Although the original brief of the Karlsborg Parachute School was to train *Fallskärmsjägare* (paratroopers), its duties were soon enlarged to include ranger-type tuition and every year, 3-400 young Swedes volunteer for service with the elite unit. Initial screening eliminates about one third of them, and the remaining candidates are submitted to a three-week battery of stringent physical and psychologial tests. Only about 100 will qualify for the 11-month course during which they will log 20-25 jumps.

The tuition at Karlsborg is broken down into three stages: basic, airborne and arctic. Basic training is followed by specialised courses (the best elements are selected for NCO and officer training). Airborne training involves eight jumps (including three by night and three in full kit) and its completion leads to the award of the first part of the qualification. The second part (airborne) is capped by the excruciating 'Eagle walk' in which trainees cover a 70km trek in 24 hours while undergoing proficiency tests (orienteering, weaponry, explosives). Those who pass are rewarded with the 'Eagle' and become fully-fledged Jaeger.

Arctic tuition takes place in the region of Borden (Norrland) and culminates in a three-week long distance raid. Conducted in winter, trainees never leave the forests and have to make the most of their survival skills.

The units trained at Karlsborg are organised into platoons subdivided into three six-Jaeger patrols (a patrol comprises two officers and six Jaegers, each a specialist in demolition, signals, intelligence or sniping). Broadly they are trained to operate in adverse surroundings for long periods.

Since 1973, courses are held every two years and attended by 10 officers and NCOs who return to their units after graduating.

In addition to Jaeger, Sweden also fields *Fallskärmsjägerskolan* (coastal Jaeger) tasked with exploring enemy held shores or disrupting hostile amphibious operations. Since 1975, the Swedish air force has its own *Basjägare* commandos.

Swedish ranger badges. From left to right and from top to bottom: early bronze badge introduced in 1952, current gold model awarded for eight jumps and the completion of the 'Eagle march'; cap badge (early model); several metal badges.

A Swedish sniper, seen in 1988 in the vicinity of Karlsborg and clad in the recently introduced camouflage outfit issued to only a few units. He is armed with the sniping version of the H&K 7.62 x 42mm assault rifle with adjustable trigger and fitted with a Schmidt and Bender scope. Regarded as the elite of Swedish forces, the Fallskärsjägare specialise in deep recce and can be compared with American rangers.

DANISH PARA-COMMANDO

*Jaegerkorps*et was descended from the Jaeger Corps, a two-battalion force created in 1785 by King Christian VII and employed throughout the 19th century for deep recce (often in small craft). In peacetime, they served as woodsmen or government clerks. Around the turn of the 20th century, the Jaeger were converted into standard infantry battalions.

The current Jaegerkorpset was formed on 1 November 1961as a recce unit operating broadly along the same lines as the British SAS. Its members attended the German airborne school until the creation of their own training centre at Alborg, Jutland, in 1964. Run like its Swedish counterpart, the school only accepts volunteers from the army, navy and air force who have served for at least a year. They first undertake the eight-week Patrol Course (Patruljeuvrus) known as Selection 1, and the few who make it proceed on to Selection 2. This test is followed by a scout swimmer course run by the Navy's Frogman Corps (Froemandskorpset), parachute, free-fall (HALO and HAHO) and specialised courses (signals, first aid, demolition etc). Other facets of training include retarded and automatic parachute jumps, combat swimming, and amphibious operations from light reconnaissance craft.

The Jaegers are then on probation for a year. It is not unusual for only one or two men to be selected per year (at one point, not one officer made it for five years!) This drastic selection is aimed at retaining only the most highly skilled personnel, capable of operating for at least 15 days in hostile surroundings, like American LRRPs. Currently, the company-sized unit is subordinate only to the Chief of Staff and comprises an HQ, training platoon (also responsible for the patrolling, selection and jump courses) maintenance and signals elements, as well as a reserve jump patrol. Interestingly, all Danish Army cadet officers must undergo the Jaegerkorpset patrol and airborne courses before commissioning with an active unit. The Danish Navy's combat diver unit also receives parachute training at the Alborg Jaeger School. ❑

A corporal of Danish Jaegerkorpset in 1989. Clad in the camouflage outfit on standard issue to Danish forces, he is equipped with a German-made, four-magazine pouch webbing. A US 1948 Model steel helmet is suspended from his belt covering the water bottle. His maroon commando beret sports the 'horn' insignia dating back to the 18th century. Armament consists of a 7.62mm M-62, the Danish-manufactured version of the German MG-3 machine-gun.

Danish Para-Commando insignia and qualification badges. From top to bottom and from left to right. Current airborne qualification badge; Air Force airborne qualification badge. Centre: variant of the current airborne qualification badge; Jaegerkorpset cap and shoulder tab badge. Various airborne qualification badges awarded to navy personnel.

NORWEGIAN PARA

In 1942, a paratroop company was formed in Great Britain from expatriate Norwegian Forces personnel. It ibecame known as the Independent Norwegian Company or F. Company. Commanded by Captain E. Dycker, F Company was sent to the Polish Parachute school in Largo House, U.K.

In 1945, the company was integrated with the 1st British Airborne Division and took part in Operation Doomsday aimed at liberating Norway. To pave the way for this operation, small parties of paratroopers were airdropped in the Trondelag region to carry out sabotage operations and to disrupt German communications. In Autumn 1945, the company was disbanded.

Simultaneously, but separately from F Company, another airborne unit was created in Scotland in 1941 and became known as the Linge Company. From 1941 onwards, this unit was celebrated for its daring seaborne and airborne attacks.The most famous of these remains the raid on the Norsk-Hydro factory at Vermosk, aimed at denying the enemy access to 'heavy water' (a component indispensable for harnessing nuclear energy). Germany's nuclear weapon development programme was dealt a crippling blow when nine members of the Linge Company destroyed the facilities producing this vital material on 27 February 1943. Throughout the war, Norwegian paratroopers worked hand in hand with local resistance forces to hamper German activities. Like F Company, this unit was also disbanded at the end of the war. For more that ten years, Norwegian High Command sees no further use in reactivating an airborne unit, and small teams or even individuals are sent abroad to train as paratroopers. Only in 1962 was the first parachutist school set up in Trandum, north of Oslo. Originally created to provide Army personnel with parachute training, it soon became identical to its Swedish model. The training provided at Sweden's Karlsberg parachute school is two-fold: to train paratroopers but also commandos, capable of carrying out reconnaissance missions behind enemy lines and guerilla activities. (In Norway such commandos are called 'Jäger'). Units from all services are sent to that school (like the Heimervernet, a territorial force trained to operate alongside Britain's 45th Royal Marines Commando). As in Sweden, the recruits are hand-picked and training is very hard. Of 200 applicants, only between 80 and 100 usually complete the gruelling 16-week course.

Training covers combat in all kinds of weather (a must in an arctic country), as well as reconnaisance and sabotage missions. At the end of their course, both officers and men are sent back to their respective services.

Norway has no airborne unit as such, apart from two airborne platoons, one operating with the North brigade, the other with Border Command troops in the Finnmark area.   ❐

NCO of the Norwegian Jäger Paratrooper Platoon on attachment to brigade North, Norway, 1990. Trained to accomplish missions ranging from reconnaissance patrols to sabotage, this para carries the standard equipment of the Norwegian army: camo uniform, chest ammo carriers, and a 7;62mm. HK 32 assault rifle with folding butt (airborne version). Identical in appearance only to conventionnal Norwegian forces this para can live off the land for months in all kinds of environment.

*Opposite:***Various Norwegian paratroop badges.**
From left to right and from top to bottom: Navy/air force metal badge (as worn on fatigue). Metal infantry badge (as worn on fatigue). Cloth shoulder patch (Airborne school) Paratrooper badge (as worn on combat uniform) Paratrooper badge (infantry version, as worn on parade dress)

DUTCH MARINIER

Raised on 10 December 1665 by Royal Decree, the Royal Dutch Naval Infantry Corps was two years later engaged successfully against the British in America when they recaptured New York - a former Dutch possession - and retained it until 1692.

During the 1900 Boxer Rebellion, the Mariniers took part in the famous siege of Beijing and 40 years later, were crushed when the German armoured steamroller swept over the Netherlands. Recreated in 1945, they were dispatched to the Far East where they reconquered the Japanese-held Dutch Indies already infested with communist guerillas. A page in the Mariniers' history was turned when Indonesia became independent in 1960. The Mariniers were repatriated and reorganised into the Koninnklijk Nederlands Korps Mariniers (KNKM) and placed under NATO Command.

Currently, KNKM fields about 2,600 men and 170 officers commanded by two field grade officers. Headquartered in Rotterdam, the force is organised into a Corps Command, responsible for Corps HQ, operations and training, Home Command responsible for the Netherlands' Defence, and Antilles Command for the protection of the Dutch Antilles. The KNKM has a very close training and wartime contingency relationship with the British Royal Marines. The Corps comprises two combat units (1 and 2 Amphibious Combat Groups or ACG) while 3 ACG (not included in total strength and to which marines completing their active service are assigned) is tasked primarily with a home defence role.

ACGs have a complement of about 700 officers and men, organised into HQ, three rifle companies, one heavy support and one services unit. Based at Doorn and a component of the Dutch Rapid Intervention Force, 1 ACG also belongs to NATO's AMF (Allied Model Force). In the latter role, it trains regularly in Norway where it would operate in wartime under the control of 3 Cdo Bde. R.M. Along with the US Marine Corps, this force constitutes NATO's amphibious force and is prepared for deployment on Europe northern and southern flanks.

Based on Curaçao and Pinta Islands in the Dutch Antilles, 2 ACG is responsible for the defence of these possessions and has thus the opportunity to conduct jungle training and joint exercises with other nations' marines in the Caribbean Islands (and in French Guiana). Mariniers participated in recent UN relief missions and were deployed in Iraqi Kurdistan (Provide Comfort in 1991) and Cambodia (1992).

A separate parachute-trained unit similar to the Brigade Patrol Troop (formerly known as the Royal Marines Mountain and Arctic Warfare Cadre), 'Whisky' Company trains extensively with 45 Cdo RM in Norway and is under its wartime operational control. The Marinier Korps also fields Co. Boat Gp, an assault craft unit specially trained in Arctic operations and paired with 359 Assault Sdn. RM. Based aboard KNS *Thetis*, the final unit is 7 Special Boat Section, made up of divers, combat swimmers and canoeists, in the same manner as its RM SBS counterpart.

The ranks of the Mariniers are made up of 80% professionals and 20% volunteer conscripts. To be commissioned with Marinier units, applicants must pass stringent psychological and medical tests (this eliminates about 60% of them). Basic training is conducted at Doorn over 16 weeks (when a further 50% will drop out) and is a prerequisite for commissioning.

From top to bottom: the 'A' model airborne qualification badge; the Marinier shoulder patch; the Corps cloth patch. Left: Marinier cap badge worn on a red background.

A Marinier of KNKM 'Whisky' Company during a 1987 exercise in Norway. Belonging to the Mariniers shock unit, this Marine Commando was pictured during manoeuvres with 45 Cdo. RM which explains his DPM combat uniform and dark blue beret cocked in British fashion. Parachute-qualified, the Marinier is also a Brigade Patrol Troop graduate. He is armed with a NATO 7.62mm FN Mag light machine-gun. Interestingly, a thick rubber roll keeps the weapon sling from cutting into his shoulder.

BELGIAN PARA-COMMANDO

On 8 May 1942, the 58 Belgian paratroopers who had qualified at Ringway in Great Britain were mustered into D Coy, 2 Belgian Paratroop Battalion and the first Commando Troop was created in August. It comprised seven officers and 100 men. Two months later, it was attached to the 10th Inter-Allied Commando, a unit composed of French, Norwegian, Polish, Dutch and British personnel. The Belgian commandos were deployed in Italy and fought from Naples to the Garigliano until January 1944. In March, the unit was attached to the 4th Commando Brigade and dispatched to the Adriatic. Meanwhile, D Coy had become the 4th Coy of the British 8th Airborne Battalion prior to being incorporated as a squadron with the SAS Brigade.

Belgian SAS teams participated in numerous intelligence missions in France and Belgium until October 1944 when the Squadron was converted into a recce unit and fought in the Netherlands. At the end of May 1945, the Squadron was expanded into 1st SAS Airborne Regiment comprising three squadrons totalling some 300 men and more than 100 vehicles. The SAS fought in Holland and Germany and were demobilised at the war's end.

The commandos of '1st Troupe' were transferred to Britain and took part in the Walcheren operation. They were engaged in Germany when the war ended. In September 1945, the unit became the Commando Regiment but its ranks were drastically reduced in the postwar years. The Schaffen Airborne School wasn't created until 1947.

Belgians paras formed the kernel of the Corps of Belgian volunteers who fought in the Korean War until 1954. On 1 September 1955, the 3rd Commando Battalion was raised at Karmina (in the Belgian Congo) and later renamed 3rd Airborne Battalion.

The Belgian paras were involved in several humanitarian missions in the Congo during that colony's struggle for independence and, in 1959, the 3rd Para Battalion reinforced by the 2nd Commando Battalion was dispached to that African territory to restore order. In July 1960, one month before the Congo's independence, the 3,000 paras of the Commando Regiment (1st, 3rd Para Battalions, 4th, 5th, 6th Commando Battalions and 11th, 13th, 14th, 15th and 16th Independent companies) made several operational jumps when riots broke out.

The Belgians evacuated the Congo in September 1960 with the exception of 3rd Para Battalion and 4th Commando which remained in Rwanda. In November 1964, troubles flared up again in the Congo prompting the Belgians to initiate Operation 'Dragon Rouge' (red dragon) involving the drop of some 320 Para-Commandos (1st Para Battalion and one company from 2nd Commando) over Stanleyville.

On 26 November, Belgian paras were dropped over Paulis when Simba insurgents threatened the population.

In 1964, the Para-Commando Regiment was inactivated and made a tactical reserve unit of the ground forces. On 28 May 1978, the paras of 1st and 2nd Battalions jumped over Kolwezi during Operation 'Red Beans' to save Europeans living in Shaba from Katanga insurgents.

Currently, the Para-Commando Regiment comprises the 1st and 2nd Airborne battalions, the 2nd Commando Battalion, backed up by one anti-tank, one artillery, and one ESR (recce) company, a recce squadron and a combat diver platoon. The basic airborne qualification badge is awarded after six aircraft and three balloon jumps. All the para-commandos train and qualify at the Commando Training Centre in Marche-les Dames, a school that also answers to the regiment. The para-commandos can truly be regarded as the elite of Belgian forces. ❏

From top to bottom and from left to right: the 'A' cloth airborne qualification badge awarded after nine jumps; the 'combat' variant; the Para-Commando metal badge; and the beret badges of the 1st, 3rd and 2nd Airborne Battalions, the 'B' and the jumpmaster qualification badges.

Autumn 1986: a sergeant of 2nd Para-Commando Battalion during an exercise in Italy. Identifiable by the green beret of 2nd and 4th Para-Commando battalions, the man wears the camouflage outfit issued to Belgian airborne forces and is armed with a Vigneron 9mm submachine-gun. With his transceiver around his neck, the man carries a smoke bomb strapped to his webbing. In his hand, he holds the ubiquitous US M1954 paratrooper helmet.

SWISS PARA

Although the creation of an airborne recce and intelligence unit specifically trained to meet the Federation's requirements had been planned by Swiss High Command since 1964, the project didn't actually get off the ground until 1967. The first cadre graduated one year later and Fallschirm-Grenadier Kompanie came into being in 1969. Commanded by Capt. Erich Grätzer, the Kompanie answered to the air force and was later designated N° 17 Long Range Scout Company (Fernspäh Kompanie). Since 1970, the training course has been run once a year, with the exception of the 1975-82 period during which it was conducted on a two-yearly basis.

Swiss youths trying out as Fernspäher must apply at age 17 and must already hold the parachute qualification awarded through the Swiss Aero Club. Screening tests are stringent, selection is merciless and on average, only about 15 from the original 300 applicants will reach the final stage. Basic tuition lasts 10 weeks and involves 10 automatic and 40 delayed jumps. The Fernspäher qualification is awarded after a further 17 week course during which students log about 130 free-falls (including 30 by night). Although they are still privates, Swiss paras have acquired all the free-fallers' tactical and technical skills when they have reached this stage. The Swiss do not have a higher level qualification even for instructors, and further experience can only be acquired by attending courses locally or in other European countries (France, Great Britain, Germany etc). Fernspäher must leave the company at age 39 as only the commanding officer is allowed to be over 40. The Grenadiers' basic training includes intensive tuition pertaining to the particular nature of their missions, such as survival in hostile surroundings, intelligence, sabotage, escape techniques etc. A one-week mountain survival test caps the final phase of training. The 17th's mission consists of advancing ahead of the unit in a hostile zone collecting intelligence data, and operating along the same lines as the US Long Range Reconnaissance Patrols.

The Grenadier paras operate in fully independent teams of 3-5 men and are issued with sophisticated equipment. According to rumour, the crash helmets of team leaders are fitted with a homing device so they can swoop straight down on the objective. Thanks to its proficiency and professionalism Switzerland's 17th Company is regarded as one of the world's first and foremost airborne units.

Swiss airborne qualification badge variants. Top: walking-out dress cloth model. Bottom: Combat fatigues cloth version. An unofficial metal model is known to be in existence.

A Swiss Airborne Grenadier of 17th Company, seen at Locarno in 1980. The man has been issued with the latest type of helmet, fitted with a camouflage cloth cover, and replacing the familiar, wide-brimmed steel helmet introduced in the prewar years. But for the chest qualification badge, nothing distinguishes this para from other Grenadiers of the Confederation. The peculiar camouflage colours are noteworthy and typical to Swiss forces, as are the combat boots with steel clamps hooked to the leather anklets. The SIG bayonet is suspended from the belt and the weapon is still the 7.62mm NATO SIG StGW 543 assault rifle. Swiss paras may only be armed with handguns for intelligence missions and often use their own, privately purchased parachutes for training jumps.

PORTUGUESE PARA

In the early 1950s, Portugal decided to emulate other European nations by creating its own airborne forces. In August 1951, one Portuguese Air Force officer and 10 NCOs were sent to Pau in southern France to qualify first as paratroopers and then later as parachute instructors.

However, another two years elapsed before instructor training resumed at Alcantarilla, Spain's parachute school. In 1955, 230 volunteers were sent to Spain for training and of that number, only 188 obtained their 'wings'. Four months later, *Batalhao Cacadores Pare-quedistas* was raised and on 26 May 1956 the formation became known as 21st Light Infantry Airborne Battalion (BCP) based at Tancos Air Base 3. In 1957, the unit expanded into a proper parachute school.

That same year, just as the first batch of trainees graduated in Portugal, another group of officers were sent to Brasil to become acquainted with the latest jump techniques as taught by the Americans.

Throughout the 1960 Portugal was forced to intervene on an increasingly massive scale to quell insurrection in her African colonies. Firstly in Angola in 1961 when open rebellion broke out giving the opportunity to send the newly-created companies of 21st BCP to Luanda, Angola. In May 1961, BCP became *Regimento Cacadores Paraque-distas* with Tancos as its rear support base. As the situation in Angola always called for more troops, extra airborne units were raised: 12th BCP (1966-74) engaged in Guinea-Bissau, 22th BCP (1962-76) based in Portugal along with 30th BCP (1962-76) and 31st and 32nd BCP based in Mozambique. At that time, 21st BCP was deployed in Angola. During their intervention in Africa, Portuguese paras made several operational jumps (though never exceeding company level).

As guerilla activities intensified, additional anti-guerilla units were raised and in 1970, special airborne groups (GEP) appeared. Made up of natives and led by Portuguese officers, these units successfully opposed the guerillas whose armament and tactics also steadily improved. Meanwhile, a deep recce airborne unit was raised in Angola. Run by the secret services and known as *'Flechas'*, it was exclusively made up of former guerillas.

In 1974-75, the Portuguese abandoned their African possessions, leading to a thorough revamping of the airborne units. The airborne regiment was disbanded and its men transferred to BETP (Base Escola de Tropas de Para).

One year later, the airborne brigade (Brigada Cacadores Para-que-dista) came into being and included BETP (Tancos), POTP1 (based in Lisboa-Monsanto) and BOTP2 (Aveiro San Jacinto). The BOTP (Base Operaciones de Tropas de Para) can be likened to an airborne rapid intervention force.

The Portuguese Navy has two airborne qualified commando groups as well as airborne underwater demolition teams.

1970: a Portuguese para corporal, during an anti-guerilla mission in Mozambique. Armed with a 7.62mm H&K light machine-gun - a remarkably efficient weapon for bush fighting - the para is clad in the camouflage uniform inspired by the French 1950 'lizard' model (of identical cut but with more faded colours). Many Portuguese officers were so impressed by the performance of French paras in Indochina and Algeria that they did everything they could to imitate them. Portuguese paras have green berets while the maroon model is exclusively issued to army commandos.

Several Portuguese insignia and qualification badges. Top: current cap badge. From left to right and from top to bottom: early badge (introduced in the 1950s); current airborne patch (introduced in 1968); commando cap badge; 1st Class badge (early model); pre-military 'half wing'; early model variant; current metal model.

SPANISH PARA

Parachuting was introduced in Spain in May 1935 when eight volunteer pilots made a demonstration jump from a Fokker-7 Trimotor aircraft over Barajas airport. During the civil war which broke out soon afterwards, both sides had their own airborne platoons with the Republicans and the Nationalists being respectively trained by Soviet and German instructors. Neither platoon, however, was deployed operationally during that conflict.

Answering to the Spanish Air Force, Spain's parachute school in Alcantarilla didn't come into being until 15 August 1947. The first batch of paratroopers graduated in 1948 and the 165 fully-fledged paras were grouped into the 1st Airborne Bandera. After the Spanish Air Force relinquished its ground forces, the Bandera was converted into an airborne squadron, a highly trained unit tasked with spearheading offensives by jumping and seizing enemy airfields and conducting guerilla actions in the enemy's rear. Organised into three sections, the Squadron was composed mostly of free-fallers and took part in numerous international training exercises alongside similar foreign units.

On 17 October 1953, Spanish Army Command decided that 1st Airborne Bandera should only be made up of Tercio legionnaires and mountain troops. Operational in April 1954, the unit was dispatched in 1956 to the Spanish Sahara and relieved in January 1957 by the 2nd Bandera which had been created in January 1956. In Morocco, paras fought insurgents and were involved in anti-guerilla warfare until February 1958.

The 29 November is a landmark in the history of Spanish paras: on that day, they made their first operational jump over Tiligiun. The 3rd Bandera was created in 1960 and five years later, High Command set up BRIPAC, Spanish Airborne Brigade.

Organised into three banderas ('Roger de Flor', 'Roger de Lauria' and 'Ortiz de Zarate'), the Brigade totals 4,700 men, and includs one airborne training and one mixed engineer battalion, with one logistics and one artillery group. Each Bandera is subdivided into five companies - three combat, one support and one services. With the exception of one Bandera deployed on a rotation basis in the Canary Islands and the training battalion based at Javali Nuevo, all these units are headquartered at Alaca de Heneraes. Paras are volunteers who serve either for 14 months with the Banderas or for 20 months with the paratroop squadrons.

The Spanish Army also has three special forces companies while a small, free-fall qualified combat diver outfit is on strength with the navy. ❐

Pictured in October 1986 in the Spanish Pyrenees, a corporal of BRIPAC's 1st Bandera. The para wears a winter jacket over his American-inspired camouflage ouifit. Badges include the subdued variant of the chest airborne qualification badge and the brigade patch on both sleeves. The silver eagle insignia of the airborne forces is worn on his black beret. His armament consists of a 9mm Parabellum Z-62 model Star submachine-gun weighing 2.65kg and firing 550rds/min.

Various Spanish airborne forces badges and insignia. From left to right and from top to bottom: Current airborne badge (combat fatigues); cap metal badge; current Number One dress airborne badge; BRIPAC shoulder patch; packer instructor badge, packer specialist badge, parachute instructor badge. (Yves Debay collection).

A para of 3rd Bandera advances cautiously towards the enemy. He is armed with a CETME LC assault rifle. Weight (empty): 3.4kg. Length (LC-86 version): 92cm. Rate of fire: 600 rds/min.

SPANISH GREEN BERET

Spaniards have always regarded guerilla warfare as an efficient way of fighting invaders and, as early as 1808, Spanish guerillas were involved in a merciless fight against Napoleon's troops. One year later, this peculiar form of warfare was officially recognised and guerilla fighters were granted the status of regular troops in time of invasion or when taking part in an uprising against enemy occupation forces.

However, it was not until 1961 that two UOEs (Unidades de Operaciones Especiales or guerillas units) were created and nominated COE 71 and 81 (Compania de las Operationes Especiales or Special Operations Companies). The first course was set up in 1965 and from then on, provided the basis for guerilla units training. Integrated with the Spanish regular forces in August 1966, these special units were tasked with guerilla and anti-guerilla warfare, and were also trained in insurgency and counter-insurgency missions. Around that time, another three units, COE 72, 41 and 62 were created. In wartime, each COE would operate on its allocated sector in compliance with DOT directives (Defensa Operativo de Territario or Operational Defence of the Territory).

In 1969, the number of UOE special units was further increased when the following COEs were formed: COE 11 (Madrid), 12 (Plasencia), 21 (Tarifa), 22 (Huelva), 31 (Alicante), 32 (Valencia), 42 (Tarragona), 51 (Zaragoza), 52 (Barbastro), 61 (Burgos), 82 (Ferrol), 91 (Granada), 92 (Ronda), 101 (Palma), and 102 (Santa Cruz). Finally COE 103 (Las Palmas) was created in 1976.

In 1979, Spanish high command decided to muster COEs into the Madrid sector and created GOE (Groupo de las Operationes Especiales or Special Operations Group) with COEs 11, 12 and 13. In 1984, GOE III (Alicante) was created by the merging of COE 31 and 32, followed in October 1985 by GOE II (Granada) comprising COE 21 and 22. In 1986 COE 51 and 52 were grouped into GOE V (Burgos), in 1987 GOE IV (Barcelona) was formed with COE 41 and 42, and finally, GOE VII (La Coruna) was created with COE 61 and 62.

In 1986, UEO was reshuffled and its forces were reorganised into three types of units, each tasked respectively with: light infantry and commando-type assignments; guerilla and anti-guerilla warfare and finally, hostage recovery, intelligence and anti-terrorism missions. Spanish volunteers wishing to obtain the green beret (worn since September 1967) must undergo two months of intensive basic training. A simulated capture followed by an interrogation bout is the final test of this phase, and the admission of the candidate depends on its outcome. Training is then pursued with various sessions in several NATO centres (officers are sent to Fort Benning in the USA) and obtaining the parachute qualification. Spanish green berets exercise regularly with their NATO counterparts and also match their skills with US Special Forces, Portuguese commandos, as well as French, Dutch, British, Belgian and German deep recce units. The operational potential of Spanish Special Forces is universally acknowledged as being one of the highest in the world. ❑

An officer of COE 31(answering to Alicante's GOE III) pictured in the winter of 1992 during an exercise in the Sierre Morena region of southern Spain. He is armed with the latest version of the 5.56mm CETME L assault rifle and clad in the camouflage outfit exclusively issued to GOE Special Forces. The rest of the equipment is standard issue to Spanish ground forces. A particular point of interest is the beret sporting both Spain's national emblem and the Spanish commandos' laurel and dagger badge.

Various badges and insignia awarded to Spanish Special forces. From left to right and from top to bottom: GEO III cloth insignia (COE 31 and 32, Alicante). Top: Special operations metal badge. Below: Special operations course metal badge; special operations course metal badge. Shoulder cloth Special Forces badge. GOE VI cloth badge (La Coruna); Special Forces high command cloth badge. COE7 badge (Answering to Alicante GOE III), and Granada GOE II cloth insignia (COE 21 and 22).

SPAIN'S FOREIGN LEGION

On 4 September 1920, the Spanish King authorised the formation of three Banderas (battalions) of the Tercio de Extranjeros (Regiment of Foreigners). General Millan Astray could be particularly pleased as he had been petitioning that Spain set up elite units ever since a treaty had been signed with France in November 1912 granting Morocco the status of a protectorate. Spanish officers and General Astray realised that an army of reluctant reservists and conscripts couldn't defeat the fierce Moroccan tribesmen. So, in 1919, the General travelled to Algeria to study the organisation of France's world-famous corps of volunteers, the legendary Foreign Legion.

On 31 October 1920, the three Banderas paraded past King Alphonso XIII and swore fidelity. On creation, the Tercio comprised a Command Headquarters, two rifle companies and one support company armed with six machine-guns, but unlike the French Foreign Legion, few actual foreigners joined the Tercios and the composition of the unit remained fairly consistent with 90% Spanish nationals.

Following its creation, the Legion was involved in the entire Moroccan campaign, and remained on African soil until 1927. The Banderas were involved in more than 850 engagements and fought from Ceuta in the west to Melilla in the east (1921-23), and from Xaiien in the south-west to Alhucemas on the Mediterranean (1924-27).

During the Spanish Civil War (1936-39), the Legion was at the spearhead of the African troops that tipped the scales in favour of the Nationalists. At that time, the Legion comprised 12 Banderas (completed by armoured companies) and distinguished itself at Madrid, Teruel and in Catalonia. Always engaged as shock troops, the Legion had lost 7,645 men killed by the time fighting ceased on 1 April 1939.

After the end of the war, 12 of the 18 Banderas were disbanded and the Legion was posted to Morocco. That country became independent in April 1956 with Spain retaining enclaves in Ceuta, Mellila, and the region south of Ifni known as as 'Spanish Sahara'. There in November 1957, the Legion fought its ultimate action on African soil when it was pitted against 2,500 well-armed fighters supported by the Moroccan government. One year later, the rebellion was crushed thanks to the co-operation of French troops in Algeria.

On 28 February 1976, Spanish Sahara ceased to exist and the Legion left the barren wastes where it had given such a good account of itself.

Currently, the Legion fields 7,000 men distributed into 1st Tercio 'Gran Capitan', 1st of the Legion and comprising the 1st, 2nd and 3rd Banderas (headquartered in Mellila); Tercio 'Duque de Alba', 2nd of the Legion - 4th, 5th and 6th Banderas (headquartered at Ceuta); Tercio 'Don Juan de Austria', 3rd of the Legion - 7th, 8th Banderas, 1st Light Cavalry Group (headquartered at Fuerteventura, Canary Islands), and 4th Tercio Alejandro de Farnesio (headquartered at Ronda).

In a royal decree of March 1986, foreigners were no longer allowed to enlist in the Legion which marked the end of a highly colourful episode of Spanish military history, but those currently serving are authorised to stay with the force until their time is up.

Composed mostly of volunteers, the ranks of the Tercios also include conscripts who have volunteered for an 18-month service. Each Bandera numbers 6-700 legionnaires, while 1st and 2nd Tercio are composed of mechanised infantry battalions. The Legion also fields three Special Forces companies, based at Ronda, the new home of the corps, and includes Unidad de Operaciones Especiales (UOE), created in 1981 and answering to 4th Tercio.

Currently, members of the Legion are deployed with UNPROFOR in Bosnia. ⌐

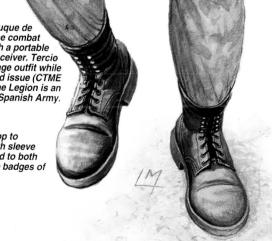

A legionnaire of 2nd Bandera, 2nd Tercio Duque de Alba, pictured in Ceuta in spring 1992. As the combat group's radio operator, he is equipped with a portable radio, as well as with the unit's HF/SSB transceiver. Tercio legionnaires are issued with a typical camouflage outfit while individual equipment and armament are standard issue (CTME assault rifle). Largely made up of volunteers, the Legion is an elite force within the Spanish Army.

Various Spanish Foreign Legion badges. From top to bottom: Unidad des Operaciones Especiales cloth sleeve insignia. Special operations course badge (issued to both Legion and ground forces). From left to right: the badges of the Legion's 1st, 2nd, 3rd and 4th Tercios.

AIRBORNE CARABINIERI

Raised in 1938 at Castel Benito near Tripoli, Italy's first airborne unit (1st Airborne Infantry Battalion) was made up initially of Libyan soldiers led by Italian officers and NCOs. This paved the way for the creation of the Tarquina Airborne School in October 1939, regarded as the cradle of Italian airborne forces which soon became the training ground of all future *'Carabinieri'*.

Officially commissioned on 1 July 1940, 1st Battalion Airborne Carabinieri numbered 22 officers, 50 NCOs and 320 all-ranks placed under the command of Major Bruto Bixio Bernadetti.

On 6 July 1941, after a year devoted to intense training and airborne tuition the Carabinieri embarked at Torento, in the south of the Italian peninsula, to be ferried to their future operational theatre in North Africa. Integrated within XXth Army Corps, they were deployed some 25km west of Tripoli, in the Suanai Ben Aden sector, to counter forays by British motorised raiding units. Between August and October 1941, the Carabinieri conducted no fewer than 220 recce missions throughout the Libyan desert.

In November their operational zone shifted towards Lamluda and Darna and the Carabinieri came up against the famous Long Range Desert Groups. They were again heavily committed when the British launched Operation 'Crusader' and, in the bitter fighting that ensued and lasted until February 1942, fought with a determination that astounded both their foes and German allies alike. On 16 March 1942, the 1st Airborne Carabinieri Battalion was then flown from Castel Benito to Rome and disbanded soon afterwards.

In the postwar years, the Italian airborne unit was only recreated on 15 May 1951 but not until 15 July 1963 was it converted into a battalion. On 1 October 1975, it was officially named 'Tuscania' 1st Airborne Carabinieri Battalion and integrated with the 'Folgore' Airborne Brigade.

'Tuscania' is mostly composed of professionals (conscripts amount to less than 20% of the force) and organised like other Italian airborne infantry units into a command and several VCC-1 APC-equipped companies. In addition to its conventional missions, 'Tuscania' is tasked with judiciary and administrative duties, can be used as riot police as well as being entrusted with purely military assignments. Heavily involved against syndicated crime (such as the Mafia and the Camorra), 'Tuscania' personnel are also trained in anti-terrorist and anti-guerilla warfare, and have operated successfully against the Red Brigades (more particularly in the days of General Della Chiesa.) Interestingly, all Special Intervention Group specialists have been provided by the 'Tuscania' Ist Airborne Carabinieri Battalion.

Carabinieri contributed contingents to most recent UN relief missions and were deployed in Kurdistan, Somalia and Mozambique. ❏

An NCO of 'Tuscania' 1st Airborne Carabinieri Battalion clad in the standard camouflage para uniform and wearing his maroon beret with the grenade-shaped Carabinieri cap badge. He is armed with a folding butt BM-59 MK III, NATO 7.62mm assault rifle. The NCO carries an M1951 9mm Beretta handgun as secondary armament.

From top to bottom. Airborne Carabinieri standard badge; 'Folgore' Division shoulder patch ('Tuscania's' mother unit); Airborne Carabinieri unofficial badge; 'Tuscania' 1st Airborne Carabinieri Battalion metal chest badge.

*Right.***Three COMSUBIN advancing along the base of a cliff during an exercise. The Italian combat divers' armament includes a Beretta 9mm automatic handgun and a smooth-bore SPAS 15 12-gauge shotgun fitted with a 6-round magazine.**
*Below.***A COMSUBIN sharpshooter takes aim with a NATO .38 Mauser SP 66 sniper rifle.**

ITALIAN COMSUBIN

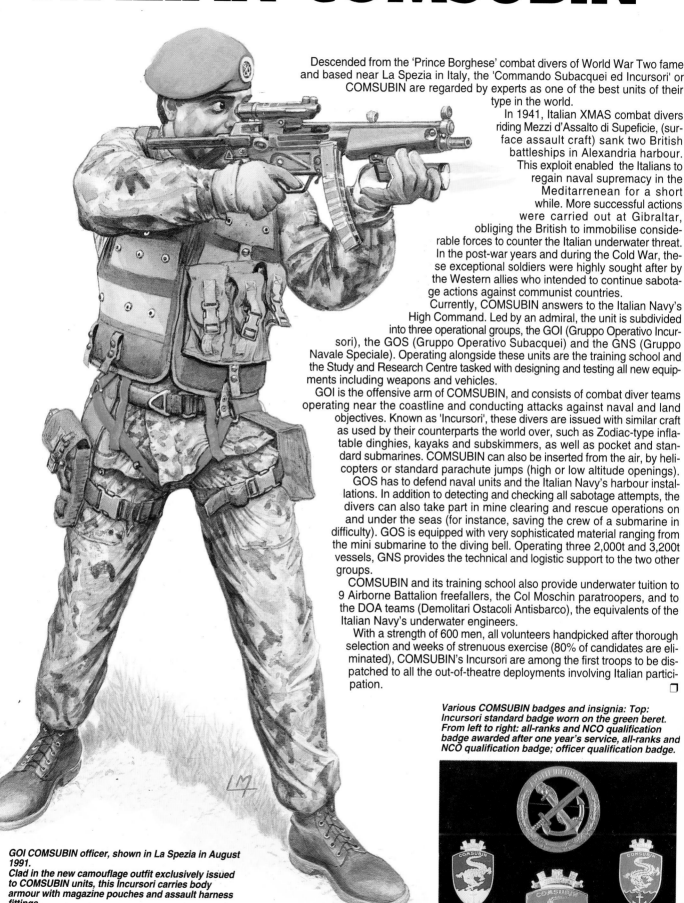

Descended from the 'Prince Borghese' combat divers of World War Two fame and based near La Spezia in Italy, the 'Commando Subacquei ed Incursori' or COMSUBIN are regarded by experts as one of the best units of their type in the world.

In 1941, Italian XMAS combat divers riding Mezzi d'Assalto di Supeficie, (surface assault craft) sank two British battleships in Alexandria harbour. This exploit enabled the Italians to regain naval supremacy in the Meditarrenean for a short while. More successful actions were carried out at Gibraltar, obliging the British to immobilise considerable forces to counter the Italian underwater threat. In the post-war years and during the Cold War, these exceptional soldiers were highly sought after by the Western allies who intended to continue sabotage actions against communist countries.

Currently, COMSUBIN answers to the Italian Navy's High Command. Led by an admiral, the unit is subdivided into three operational groups, the GOI (Gruppo Operativo Incursori), the GOS (Gruppo Operativo Subacquei) and the GNS (Gruppo Navale Speciale). Operating alongside these units are the training school and the Study and Research Centre tasked with designing and testing all new equipments including weapons and vehicles.

GOI is the offensive arm of COMSUBIN, and consists of combat diver teams operating near the coastline and conducting attacks against naval and land objectives. Known as 'Incursori', these divers are issued with similar craft as used by their counterparts the world over, such as Zodiac-type inflatable dinghies, kayaks and subskimmers, as well as pocket and standard submarines. COMSUBIN can also be inserted from the air, by helicopters or standard parachute jumps (high or low altitude openings).

GOS has to defend naval units and the Italian Navy's harbour installations. In addition to detecting and checking all sabotage attempts, the divers can also take part in mine clearing and rescue operations on and under the seas (for instance, saving the crew of a submarine in difficulty). GOS is equipped with very sophisticated material ranging from the mini submarine to the diving bell. Operating three 2,000t and 3,200t vessels, GNS provides the technical and logistic support to the two other groups.

COMSUBIN and its training school also provide underwater tuition to 9 Airborne Battalion freefallers, the Col Moschin paratroopers, and to the DOA teams (Demolitari Ostacoli Antisbarco), the equivalents of the Italian Navy's underwater engineers.

With a strength of 600 men, all volunteers handpicked after thorough selection and weeks of strenuous exercise (80% of candidates are eliminated), COMSUBIN's Incursori are among the first troops to be dispatched to all the out-of-theatre deployments involving Italian participation. ❏

Various COMSUBIN badges and insignia: Top: Incursori standard badge worn on the green beret. From left to right: all-ranks and NCO qualification badge awarded after one year's service, all-ranks and NCO qualification badge; officer qualification badge.

GOI COMSUBIN officer, shown in La Spezia in August 1991.
Clad in the new camouflage outfit exclusively issued to COMSUBIN units, this Incursori carries body armour with magazine pouches and assault harness fittings.
He is armed with a 9mm HK MP-5A3 submachine-gun, the handguard of which is fitted with a powerful flashlight. The two magazines taped together for quick reloading are noteworthy. In addition to the gasmask strapped to the thigh, each COMSUBIN is issued with a 9mm Para 92 SB Beretta handgun.

61

GREEK PARA

Greek Para-Commandos are heirs to the famous parachute-trained 'Sacred Battalion' raised in 1942 with British assistance and composed exclusively of former regular officers. Its 150 members conducted raids with the SAS in North Africa and operated alongside the SBS in the Aegean. Later, the 'Sacred Battalion' was attached to the New Zealand Corps before being integrated with General Leclerc's Free French where they were issued with 30 jeeps for raids against the Axis forces in Tunisia. In the war years, the Battalion was commanded by Colonel Tsigantes who had fought at Bir Hakeim alongside the Free French. After the surrender of Axis forces in Tunisia, the Battalion was transferred to Egypt and attached to the Special Boat Service.

On 31 October 1943, 200 Greek commandos jumped over Sarnios Island in a combined airborne amphibious operation (the rest of the battalion was delivered by destroyer). The attack however met with limited success. In February 1944, the 1st Squadron was fighting the Germans in the Aegean. Two months later, the 450 members of the unit were sent for airborne training to the British Airborne School at Ramta, in Palestine, before fighting in the Dodecanese in 1944.

On 2 April 1945, the Greeks were integrated with British special forces and took part in Operation 'Ted' against Rhodes and Alimna. The Battalion was disbanded shortly after the end of the war.

In 1955, a US-advised jump school was created outside Athens and training was entrusted to American Special Forces. One year later, the graduates were sent to Fort Benning to attend the Instructor and Ranger courses. Greek para-commandos were modelled on their US counterparts and used their training methods. In 1965, three para-commando battalions had been raised and commisioned into the 2nd Parachute Regiment of the 3rd Special Forces Division. This para-commando division included a three-battalion airborne regiment and one special forces battalion. The commando regiment comprised three commando battalions and one naval infantry unit (three battalions). The Greek Navy also has a parachute-trained combat diver unit.

Each regiment fields an airborne artillery battalion and support units. The Greek Special Forces Battlion is composed of independent four-man teams, exclusively tasked with deep recce behind enemy lines. Regarded as the elite of Hellenic forces, the Greek paras are all volunteers who also train in mountain warfare. ❑

1988: Greek para-commando of the 3rd Special Forces Brigade, 1st Commando Regiment. Wearing the camouflage combat uniform typical of para-commando units, the man is armed with the airborne folding butt version of the Belgian-made FAL assault rifle. The numerous ammo pouches are noteworhty. The green beret is also representative of Para-Commando units.

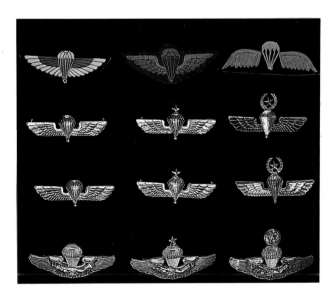

*From top to bottom and from left to right: **Early World War 2 model; 1955 version; British-inspired model; basic qualification badge, senior badge, jumpmaster badge; and four variants of the previous models (free-fall, basic, senior and jumpmaster).***

WARSAW PACT

 **EAST GERMANY**

 **CZECHOSLOVAKIA**

 **POLAND**

 **YUGOSLAVIA**

SOVIET UNION

EAST GERMAN PARA

Although East Germany's Nationale Volksarmee was raised in 1956, the 5th Fallschirmjägerbataillon (parachute battalion) numbering 250 men didn't come into being until 1962.

The unit was trained by the Soviets - who then controlled the East German forces - and by a handful of World War 2 veterans. Within 10 years, the Battalion changed its name twice: first designated 2nd Battalion, it was then in 1973 given the name of a German communist hero and became officially known as 40th Airborne Battalion 'Willi Sanger' (40. 'Willi Sanger' Fallschirmjäger Bataillon). It is under this new name that the Battalion appeared in the 1973 NVA order of battle.

Quartered at Proro on Rugen Island, in the Baltic Sea, the Battalion was regarded by foreign observers as one of the most professional fighting units of the Warsaw Pact, second only to the famous Spetsnaz. The Battalion did not answer to the Military District Command but was controlled directly by East Germany's Ministry of Defence. In the 1970s, most of its members took part in all the foreign ventures Moscow was involved in (Syria and Ethiopia in 1979) or served as advisors with the Ethiopian airborne forces. Reportedly, these specialists ran and controlled all the radio transmission services in Libya, Ethiopia and Angola.

Unlike other Warsaw Pact airborne forces, the 40th Battalion never had heavy equipment and, in wartime, would have primarily been tasked with recce and sabotage missions behind NATO lines. For these assignments, the Battalion would have split into several 4-12 man teams, clad like Bundeswehr regulars and waging unconventional warfare in the same way as World War 2 Skorzeny's Commandos.

In true German fashion, training was intensive and thorough, with the emphasis placed on top physical shape and proficiency in commando and demolition skills.

In addition to the para battalion, East German High Command could rely on highly specialised deep recce groups modelled on the Soviet 'Reydoviki' and answering only to the Ministry of State Security (East German equivalent of the KGB).

The Volksmarine (Navy) had a number of Kampfschwimmer (combat swimmer) companies, parachute-trained and intended to support amphibious operations or for raiding. With some of them free-fall qualified, the Kampfschwimmer were conversant with explosive disposal and combat demolition techniques. ❐

An Unterfeldwebel (corporal) of East Germany's 40th Parachute Battalion. The 400 Fallschirmjäger of this unit were dressed in the standard camouflage uniform on issue to all NVA forces. He is armed with the ubiquitous 7.62mm AK-47 assault rifle later superseded by the 5.45mm AK-74. The camouflage ammo pouch, the AK-47 bayonet and the gas mask container are suspended from the belt. Not visible here is the crash helmet (also worn in combat) and replaced when off duty by the maroon beret worn with orange collar tabs. The cap badge is shown as well as the unit patch on the left sleeve.

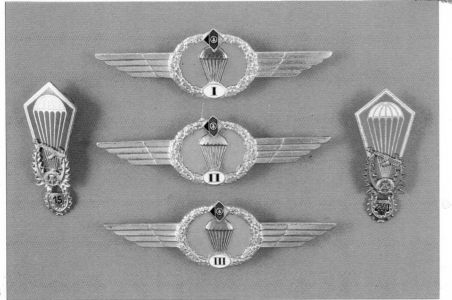

East German airborne qualification badges. Central row (from top to bottom). The three 1959-63 airborne proficiency level badges (this type was phased out in 1965). Left and right: later variants indicating the number of jumps (initially silver, these badges were later gilded).

YUGOSLAV PARA

Although parachuting was introduced in Yugoslavia as early as 1928, army circles took no heed of the military potential of this new sport until 1940 when German paras intervened so dramatically in the Netherlands and Belgium. To make up for lost time, Belgrade initiated an airborne training programme and 50 members of the air force were selected for the first course at Zemun airfield, near Belgrade. Simultaneously, a further 40 officers attended a similar course at Pencebo, 19km south of the capital city, (only the qualification badges differentiated the graduates).

The German invasion of Yugoslavia in 1940 brought the training programme to a momentary halt.

Yugoslav airborne-activities resumed in August 1944 when 100 partisans were sent to Bari in Italy to be trained by British instructors. All of them qualified after eight jumps and were sent back to Yugoslavia on 6 January 1944 to form the cadre of a para battalion. During the war, numerous officers and NCOs of the Royal Yugoslav Army were dropped individually over their country for sabotage and recce missions.

The war ended and, by 1947, British training methods were superseded by those of the Soviet 'Big Brother' and from then on, Yugoslav paras were trained in Soviet jump techniques and equipment. By 1950, the original para battalion had grown into a three-battalion brigade, one of which was turned into a training unit and designated 36th Brigade.

In Soviet fashion, a youth organisation was created to provide parachute tuition and served as a crucible for the training of would-be paras.

This pre-training also allowed for the selection of the best elements. Composed of army personnel, the Airborne Brigade answers to air force command and is regarded as the elite of Yugoslav forces. Handpicked after stringent selection, all paras are volunteers who obtain their 'wings' after 10 jumps.

Based at Nis, the Brigade also fields several sections of free-fallers with a heavy company armed with recoilless guns and mortars. The Yugoslav army also has a mountain brigade specialising in guerilla warfare and a naval infantry brigade controlled by the navy.

Although the Yugoslav conflict has now been raging for two years, the Federal Army still boasts a substantial complement of special forces, and this in spite of purges, eliminations and desertions. True, their ranks have been replenished by a steady influx of volunteers (mainly Serbs) but it looks as though the Belgrade authorities will commit their crack units only if the situation becomes really desperate.

So far, only half a company of the 36th Airborne Brigade has been involved in combat when dispatched in June 1991 to relieve a border guard unit cornered by Slovenes along the Italian border. When war broke out, the Federal Army had nine special forces brigades, each comprising three battalions. 36th Airborne Brigade was made up of three combat battalions, three command companies, plus light support and deep recce companies.

According to unspecified sources, the Brigade has now been disbanded and its members deployed in Bosnia and Croatia to command reservists.

❒

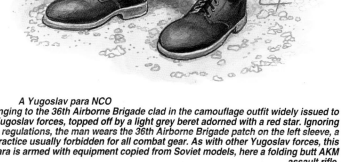

A Yugoslav para NCO
belonging to the 36th Airborne Brigade clad in the camouflage outfit widely issued to Yugoslav forces, topped off by a light grey beret adorned with a red star. Ignoring regulations, the man wears the 36th Airborne Brigade patch on the left sleeve, a practice usually forbidden for all combat gear. As with other Yugoslav forces, this para is armed with equipment copied from Soviet models, here a folding butt AKM assault rifle.

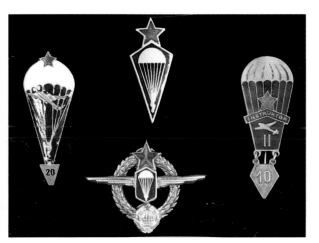

Yugoslav airborne qualification badges. From top to bottom and from left to right: variant of the current badge; army badge awarded for 20 jumps; 1970s' instructor badge; early instructor badge issued in the 1950s.

Various types of weapon issued to the Polish Assault Brigade presented by recce special intervention commandos. From top to bottom and from left to right: A member of GRN armed with a one-shot 40mm light grenade launcher.

A para equippped with a 5.45mm Tantal, the Polish-made version of the AK-47. In the centre, a crossbow used to kill sentries. A special forces soldier armed with a hatchet. A commando equipped with a bow.

POLISH PARA

The Poles were as far sighted as the Soviets when they decided as early as 1936 to set up an airborne force and had a jump tower built at the Ostrox-Mazowiecka Infantry School. Meanwhile, on 23 September, Polish instructors made their first balloon jumps over Jablona in the vicinity of Warsaw.

One year later, the 60 instructors of the test unit made several demonstration jumps during a manoeuvre at Wieliszewe. The airborne platoon was ready in 1938 and displayed its skills in the annual major exercises staged by the Polish Army. In May 1939, an airborne school was created at Bydgoszoz, but only one batch of trainees graduated before the German invasion interrupted the training programme.

Overcoming many hurdles, numerous Polish paras found their way to embattled Britain and in September 1941, the 1st Polish Parachute Brigade came into being while a training centre exclusively for Polish personnel was set up in Scotland. The Brigade was incorporated with the 1st Allied Airborne Brigade in June 1944 but took no part in the Normandy landings.

The Poles had to wait until Operation 'Market Garden' at Arnhem to make their first operational jump. In this action, part of the Brigade was delivered by gliders on 18 and 19 September 1944, and the remainder of the unit was dropped two days later over the inferno. Led by General Sosabowski (who was staunchly personally opposed to the operation), the Poles held the Waal and Maas bridges. They suffered staggering losses with only 160 men out of the original 2,200 making it back across the Rhine to the Allied lines.

Meanwhile, the Russians raised a Polish airborne assault battalion and used it for recce missions behind German lines.

Based in Germany until 1947, the Brigade was disbanded and not recreated until 1957 when it became designated as 6th 'Pomerania' Air Assault Division (6 PDPD).

Based in the vicinity of Krakow, 6th 'Pomarska' totalled 6,000 men, trained in all facets of special operations and conventional warfare. Distributed into four airborne and one SF battalion, the unit was not heavily mechanised as it lacked airdroppable vehicles and was issued with OT-64 SKOTs instead of MBDs.

Polish paras obtained their 'wings' after seven jumps (200 for instructors) and because of their sheer professionalism (shared with East Germans, Czechs and Hungarians) used to look down on Russians paras with some contempt.

Reportedly, Polish and Russian paras were ready to seize Paradubitz Airport during the 1968 Soviet intervention in Czechoslovakia.

Operating independently from the 6th Airborne Division and answering to the intelligence service, 410th Airborne Battalion was composed of free-fallers who were assigned the most daring and dangerous missions. ❏

Only his maroon beret differentiates this 'starszy chorazy' (warrant officer) of 6th PDPD from standard Polish Forces. Clad in the current field service uniform, the man is armed with an PM 63 machine pistol and wears its holder and pouch. The Polish silver braid eagle is worn centrally on the beret, above his rank insignia (three stars). The latter is repeated on the shoulder strap. The parachute instructor badge is worn above the right breast pocket.

From left to right and from top to bottom: standard patch issued to Polish forces in Britain (1940-44) and worn on the headgear; collar badge of British-trained paras; 1st Polish Brigade qualification badge; badge awarded for an operational jump ('Arnhem'); Soviet-inspired postwar airborne qualification badge; current airborne qualification badge (silver model indicating the number of jumps: 15, 25, 50, 75 and 100); instructor badge with wreath and number of jumps. In the 1970s, World War 2 models were reintroduced for army personnel. For a number of years, the number of jumps on free-faller instructor badges has been replaced by proficiency levels III, II and M.

70

CZECH PARA-COMMANDO

On the night of 28 December 1941, a four-engined Halifax bomber took off from Britain and set course for Nazi-occupied Czechoslovakia. On board were seven Czech paras, organised into three teams who were about to be dropped over their home country. Their mission was to murder Reinhard Heydrich, chief of the Gestapo and 'protector' of Bohemia and Moravia. The agents carried out their mission successfully but were tracked down and killed by the Germans who avenged Heydrich's death with savage reprisals. The Czech paras had fought their first battle.

Throughout the war, Czechs were trained in Great Britain and carried out diversion, recce and sabotage missions, while in the East, Soviet High Command raised a Czech Airborne Brigade, numbering more than 2,700 men and women levied from the 1st Czech Army, then engaged alongside the Soviets. After training, the Brigade was deployed operationally in September 1944 and attached to the 1st Ukrainian Front in the Carpathians where they fought as infantry. On 25 September, the Brigade was dropped over a salient held by Slovak insurgents but gradually yielded to German pressure. At the end of November, the Czechs withdrew into the mountains and fought like partisans until March 1945 when they were repatriated home and reorganised into an infantry unit.

In 1946, Czech High Command raised 22nd Vysadkova Brigada (22nd Airborne Brigade) at Prostejev. In addition to its conventional role, the Brigade could also be tasked with more complex missions such as deep recce and sabotage missions thanks to a special 'raiders' unit based at Holesov. In the 1960s, motorised divisions were strengthened by an airborne recce unit. The 1968 Soviet intervention in Czechoslovakia was followed by a severe purge resulting in drastic cuts in the ranks of the Brigade.

A regiment-sized unit, 22nd Vysadkova Brigade is based in the vicinity of Prosnice and fields one active, one reserve and one training battalion (the fourth specialises in special missions and operates along the same lines as the Russian Spetsnaz). All these battalions have their own organic support units. As with East German units, Czech airborne battalions are organised as standard airborne infantry, issued with their own armoured vehicles and anti-tank armament.

In the days of the Warsaw Pact, Czech paras were volunteers, chosen from the Communist Youth Movement or from the Svarzam pre-military organisation. Political conviction was regarded then as an important recruiting criteria.

The Check Republic retained most of the Brigade when Czechoslovakia was partitioned in 1993 and, but for a few para units, Slovakia has practically no airborne force. ❐

A corporal of Czechoslovakia's 22nd Airborne Brigade during a 1986 exercise. Worn as a substitute for the typical Czech 1965 Pattern camouflage uniform, the man's combat outfit is practically identical to models issued to former Warsaw Pact forces. The crash helmet is made of synthetic material while the brownish grey beret is tucked into his belt. The para is armed with a folding butt VZ-58 assault rifle, the Czech-made version of the Soviet AKM.

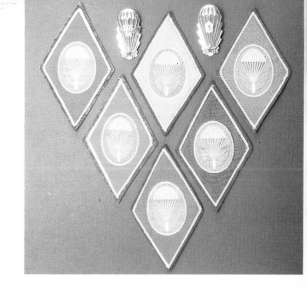

Czech insignia and airborne qualification badges. From left to right and from top to bottom. 22nd Airborne Brigade Anti-tank Group badge; 1965 instructor metal badge; 22nd Brigade standard badge; tactical recce group badge; deep recce unit badge; command and support group badge; airborne training unit badge.

SOVIET PARA

Like all elite soldiers, Soviet paras were more motivated than other Red Army soldiers and justly proud of belonging to the cream of Moscow's forces.

In the 1930s, the Soviets were the first to pioneer airborne operations and in 1935, foreign observers were astonished when 2,500 paras jumped over Kiev during manoeuvres. In spite of Stalin's bloody purges through the ranks of the Red Army, in 1939 the Reds fielded three fully operational airborne brigades which were dropped over Finland that November.

During World War 2, only two airborne operations were carried out and both ended in total failure, resulting in Soviet paras fighting only as elite infantry until the end of the conflict.

New Soviet offensive doctrines initiated in the 1950s saw the rebirth of airborne units while, in the 1970s, the introduction of the airdroppable BMD armoured vehicle gave their firepower a considerable boost.

The 1968 invasion of Czechoslovakia heralded a period of success for the Soviet paras when 103th Guards Division and GRU (the Soviet Army's intelligence service) seized Prague Airport. Some two hours later, the paras' ASU-85 took up position in front of the Party Building in the centre of the Czech capital city.

In 1977 VDV paras (Vozdushno Desantnye Vojska or independent airborne force) , intermingled with Cuban and Ethiopian units were engaged successfully in the African peninsula and repelled the Somalis into the Ogaden desert.

Always at the spearhead, the 105th Airborne Division led the initial assault on Kabul during the 1979 invasion of Afghanistan. As the Afghan capital city was torn apart by rival factions, Soviet paras were in the thick of the fighting, reducing all strongholds with their armour and heavy artillery.

Then, during the Yom Kippur War, 103rd Airborne Guards Division was kept on full readiness, waiting for the order to be dispatched to the Middle East in support of the Arabs.

With their organisation and structure practically unchanged since the days of the Soviet regime, Russian airborne divisions total about 700 officers and 6,500 men, backed up by 300 airdroppable BMD APCs (although some specialised units are issued with ASU-87 self-propelled guns). Used as a tactical reserve or deployed within Russia's rapid intervention force, VDV airborne assault divisions consist of three airborne regiments, one air defence battalion, one artillery regiment, one engineer battalion, one signals battalion, one recce company, one NBC defence company, one transport battalion, one maintenance battalion and one medical battalion.

Training is tough, and the Russian para hardly gets any leave at all during his three-year service, but his lot will improve if he signs up for an extended period with the force. His standard individual armament is the 5.45mm AK-74 assault rifle, the folding butt version of the ubiquitous Kalashnikov, improved by the addition of a muzzle brake that funnels most of the blast sideways, thus reducing recoil, improving accuracy and increasing the rate of fire.

Russian airborne units have a substantial allotment of light machine-guns (RPK-74s) and rely on RPG-16, RPG-18 and SPG-9 for anti-tank warfare. Although its range is limited, the AGS-17 grenade launcher is still highly praised, while air defence is entrusted to 23mm ZU-33 twin anti-aircraft guns and SA-7/16 Grail anti-aircraft missiles.

Early 1980s: a Soviet VDV paratrooper in summer camouflage combat dress and armed with a scope fitted SVD 7.62mm Dragunov sniper rifle. Under the camouflage coveralls adopted by the ground forces in the 1970s, the striped shirt typical of Soviet elite forces can be seen. In the 1960s and for a limited period, the VDV paras wore the red beret but soon reverted to their blue headgear indicating their close ties with the air force. In VDV units, sniper rifles are available in larger quantities than in comparable western formations. Webbing and magazine pouches are standard issue to airborne forces.

Soviet airborne badges. From left to right: instructor badge (awarded for 100 jumps and available in 200, 300 etc versions); advanced badge (10-100 jumps) and basic badge (1-10 jumps). Far right: airborne assault troops shoulder patch. Above: two versions of the metal collar insignia.

RUSSIAN SPETSNAZ

Western intelligence services did not even suspect the existence of Spetsnaz units until the 1980s when a defecting Soviet officer revealed that highy trained special forces were operating within the Red Army. According to him, these special units were composed of exceptional elements whose wartime assignments included the disruption of NATO's rear, the sabotage of key strategic points and the elimination of political and military leaders. The mysterious Spetsnaz soon became the bogey of (Although the Spetsnaz threat will never be accurately assessed, it now appears that they never were quite as fiendish as the West let itself think) Western High Command and the top Soviet agents were reported everywhere.

The forerunners of Spetsnaz were World War 2 Soviet airborne commandos who fought throughout the 'Great Patriotic War' in German-occupied territories, cutting the enemies' communication lines and contributing through their action to the immobilization - and eventual annihilation - of numerous Axis divisions.

This concept of commando troops fighting in the enemy's rear was perpetuated through the 1950s and led to special units being commissioned with each Soviet front-line division. Mostly made up of parachute-trained volunteers, these units were tasked with infiltrating enemy lines (or parachuting behind them) so as to sabotage communications, or conduct limited scale attacks and hold out until reinforcements arrived. After joining up with friendly forces, Spetsnaz would be redeployed forward again for another similar mission. Soviet top brass was aware that Spetsnaz losses would be staggering but, in true Red Army fashion, showed more concern for success than soldiers' lives.

Officially, the Spetsnaz' first action took place in 1968 when these elite soldiers paved the way for Soviet intervention in Czechoslovakia. On the night of 20 August, several teams were airlanded by Aeroflot Antonov 24s into Prague airport and secured it until the arrival of the 103rd Guards Airborne Division.

Some 11 years later, on 24 December, about 100 Spetsnaz were among the Soviet soldiers who took over Bagram Airport in the early stages of the Soviet deployment in Afghanistan. Along with KGB special intervention teams, Spetsnaz agents were tasked with seizing the presidential residence and liquidating the Afghan Communist Party's General Secretary, Babrak Karmal. The mission was successful and from then on, Spetsnaz were increasingly committed in the field.

Until the Red Army pulled out in February 1989, Soviet Command called on Spetsnaz units increasingly frequently to break the back of Mujaheedin resistance. Putting their harsh training into practice, small parties infiltrated insurgent-held areas where they were relayed by air (drops or helicopters), and conducted raids, sabotage action and systematically eliminated Afghan resistance leaders. Their brilliant successes however had little bearing on the course of events and could not prevent the Red Army from progressively bogging down in the Afghan quagmire. As the war went on, the Mujaheedins' armament and tactics steadily improved and it soon became clear that only commando-type Spetsnaz units could effectively operate in rugged surroundings where cumbersome armoured formations, ill-suited to the ground configuration, found their crushing firepower useless.

The Afghan War gave Spetsnaz a substantial boost and in the late 1980s, each of the 40 Soviet Armies had its own 'Spets' company. There was also one brigade for each of the 16 Military Command, while a further four, more specifically trained for waterborne action, were commissioned with the Fleets. In addition, an airborne Spetsnaz battalion was under direct airborne command. Brigades ranged from 1,000 to 1,300 men distributed into 100-man sub-units and mostly staffed with conscripts (although more specialised staff such as 'elimination' teams or combat divers were and are still recruited exclusively from among career personnel).

Unlike their naval counterparts who came out unscathed when the ex-Red Army elements were redistributed among the other republics, the Spetsnaz were badly affected by the disappearance of the Red Army which led to some of their units being disorganised - not to say disbanded. Until 1991, eight Spetsnaz brigades were on strength with ground forces while one was attached to the airborne divisions. According to recent estimates, only the 'Spets' battalion, quartered near Moscow, and 5th and 7th Brigades are known to be still in existence. The fate of the others is unknown. This can be traced back to two causes: firstly, the majority of Spetsnaz officers originated from Russia and have returned to their homeland, and secondly, the brigades were mostly staffed with conscripts who have chosen to return to the republics they were drafted from.

Many 'Spets' are serving as mercenaries in other republics, while others have returned to civilian life after finding that activities such as close protection or security offer a far more lucrative living than the armed forces. Only 2-5,000 Spetsnaz from the 15-18,000 the Red Army once fielded are known to be still active. ❑

A Spetsnaz NCO of Moscow's Special Forces Airborne Battalion in autumn 1992. A professional soldier, he is armed with a sound-suppressed 9 x 18mm Makarov automatic pistol. Also known as P-6 or P-B, the weapon's magazine holds 8 rounds and is fitted with a silencer that must be thoroughly cleaned after 20 shots. In addition to his handgun, the Spetsnaz is equipped with a 5.45mm AKSU-74 submachine-gun, a compact weapon well suited to the tasks of special forces agents. His camouflage outfit is typical of airborne forces.

Spetsnaz unit badges. Left: Airborne battalion badge (Moscow Command). Right: badge issued to one of the Higher Ryazan Airborne Command School units.

MVD SPETSNAZ

Since its creation, the Soviet Ministry of the Interior (MVD) has always disposed of its own combat units. Known as OPNAZ (Operativny Naznacherie), these lightly-armed forces field 200,000 militiamen and well into the eighties have constituted the stong arm of MVD. Today, the kernel of this crack unit is the 10,000-men strong Djerzhinsky motorised division.

The bulk of these forces were used to guard the prison camps (gulags), jails or government offices. But in the mid eighties, the upsurge of nationalism in the Soviet republics emphasized the need for specialised troops capable of handling-riot or anti-terrorist duties. Hurriedly, more credits were made available to finance the establishment of new OPNAZ-controlled intervention units. Known as OMON (Otryad Milistii Osobog Naznacheniya) these militia units were entrusted with special tasks and became notorious for their black berets. From 1987 to 1988, OMON units were simultaneously created in Moscow, Leningrad, Kiev, Minsk and Novosibirsk. Their commander was General Yuri Shatalin (appointed in 1986, he is still in command today). To cope with a quickly deteriorating situation in the Soviet Union, Shatalin successfully developed a 36,000 man-force, including 18,000 men operating in intervention units. These were known as MVD Spetsnaz, or MVD special forces. In the wake of a decision taken by the Supreme Soviet on 4 August 1989, OMON was entrusted with *'fighting crime at a higher level'*. New weapons, uniforms and equipment were purchased including 4x4 light trucks, armoured vehicles and lorries. But more important, recruiting was no longer so selective. It was aimed mostly at 'de-mobbed' soldiers, more particularly Afghanistan veterans, where Shatalin himself had served. He knew that he could rely on these men. To make enlisting more attractive, better pay and improved family conditions were offered to those volunteers who were not only enticed by action and adventure.

Besides, the Soviet government decided to provide OMON with its own helicopters, improved signals and a special air fleet, permenantly detached from the Red Air Force, to enable quick airlifting to trouble areas.

In 1989, as these units were being formed, incidents broke out in the Transcaucasian republics. MVD resorted to all possible means to restore order and MVD cadets were sent to Uzbekistan and Georgia. In 1989 and for the first time since their return from Afghanistan, OMON units were sent from Moscow to Tbilisi in Georgia where they were used alongside paratroops. Then, they intervened again in Kirgiz with KGB troops and the 15th Armoured Division. In October 1991, OPNAZ numbered 26,700 men, and their ranks included the mysterious OMSN (Otryad Milistii Spetsial'nogo Naznacheniya), the Militia Special Intervention Group. Under this unconspicuous denomination operate the MVD anti-terrorist units, identical to France's GIGN or to Germany's GSG-9. Their origin dates back to 1977, when on 31 December of that year, MVD decided to create an anti-terrorist unit in anticipation of the 1980 Olympic Games. Commanded by Captain Malstev, these units were modelled on their Western counterparts, such as the American Delta Force or GSG-9. They intervened for the first time in 1982 during a hostage seizure.

Today, OMSN has grown stronger, with its establishment reaching an estimated level of 2,500 to 3,000 men. Distributed among ten units, its members operate in close co-operation with OPNAZ throughout the Soviet Union's trouble spots. Russian-born in their majority, OMSN members are all volunteers. Handpicked, they must undergo rigorous psychological and physical tests to gain admission into this elite force.. ❐

OMSN NCO.(Militia Special Intervention Platoon). High Karabahk, January 1991: with their missions identical to anti-terrorist units, they operated in the Caucasus to keep apart the Azeri and Armenian communities. To be less conspicuous, OMSN gear was identical to the new MVD's OPNAZ combat units,with the red beret the only difference. OMSN wear the same combat uniform as KGB and Red Army elite troops. The bullet- proof jacket features chest pouches and is held by a leather belt. Extra padding is worn to protect the legs against projectiles during violent protests. This OMSN is armed with a 5,45mm AK-47. Two magazines are taped together for quicker re-loading, a common practice among Western forces. The man also wears leather mittens for improved grip.

Opposite. From left to right:
Various MVD combat unit badges:
OPNAZ beret badge, MVD unit cloth shoulder patch,
and badge beret. Originally, this badge was worn by
paratroopers and marines only, but in recent times, its
use has become widespread among OPNAZ units.

SOVIET MARINE

Although a relatively small unit when compared with other elite forces, the Soviet naval infantry is heir to a long tradition dating back to 1705 when Czar Peter the Great raised a marine regiment to serve with his imperial fleet. Disbanded after the Napoleonic wars, the regiment was replaced by temporary marine companies and served in the 19th and 20th century wars in the Crimea and against Japan.

The advent of communism changed little and the new marine brigade was not created until 1940 when it was commissioned with the Baltic Fleet.

The strength of Soviet naval infantry reached a peak during World War 2 with the force fielding more than 350,000 men, organised into 40 brigades, 6 independent regiments and numerous special units. For their bravery during the conflict, five of these brigades were granted Guards status. In the postwar years, the role of the marines was considerably reduced and the force was eventually disbanded. It was recreated in 1961 when Soviet Naval Command decided to raise naval infantry units and allocate them to the North Sea, Black Sea and Pacific Fleets. Each fleet thus received its own brigade while naval infantry detachments were attached to smaller flotillas (Sea of Azov, Danube etc.)

Each brigade comprised three naval infantry and one armoured battalion, although each brigade's complement could be boosted significantly in wartime. As for the motorised battalions, they were equipped with 35 BTR-70 APCs each (these vehicles being gradually superseded by BTR-80s). Armoured battalions were issued with 35 amphibious PT-76s and 10 T-72s, although some units still have T-55s. Thanks to a reorganisation and updating process initiated in 1982, Soviet naval infantry units were endowed with greater firepower after the introduction of BM-21 multiple rocket launchers, ZSU-24/4 self-propelled guns, SA-8 Gecko anti-aircraft missiles, and M-74 122mm artillery pieces. Lighter armament was also issued, such as Spigot anti-tank missiles and AGS-17 grenade launchers.

Totalling 18,000 men, the Soviet naval infantry was a relatively small force and amounted to only one tenth of its American equivalent, the USMC. The missions of the Black Berets, however, were more modest and consisted only in landing and striking in the enemy's rear or seizing a strategic objective. Their tactics also differed from those of the 'Leathernecks' who, as demonstrated in the Pacific War against the Japanese, always have had sufficient power and means to bring a massive force ashore in the face of a well-entrenched foe. Although because of the sheer size of their naval infantry force the Soviets could have never competed with the Americans on equal terms, they made significant headway in the use of air-cushion vehicles, the largest of which can carry up to 220 marines or four PT-76s and two T-72s. At home over ground or water, these craft are capable of breaching enemy defence lines and allow for rapid movement of troops.

As carefully selected as the paras, Soviet marines used to be handpicked from the best by Soviet Navy officers in recruiting sessions held throughout the country. Each service used to have its own recruiting quota and after several months of intensive training (all officers and NCOs were career staff), the new marines were commissioned with a fleet. There, they had to display the same proficiency in both their sailor and infantryman roles, while still serving in an elite corps proud of its black beret. ❑

From left to right: beret metal badge (all ranks); marine sleeve insignia, Soviet navy metal badge worn on the beret next to the marine badge.

Summer 1986: a captain of Soviet naval infantry of the Baltic Fleet during an exercise in the vicinity of Leningrad. The man is clad in the black summer outfit typical of Soviet Naval Infantry forces. Shortly afterwards, all Soviet marines were issued with camouflage uniforms. As indicated by the chest airborne qualification badge, the Marine is parachute-trained. He carries a leather map case, and his weapon is the unusual Stechkin handgun, a 9 x 18 mm wooden butt handgun capable of firing bursts.

MIDDLE EAST

TURKEY

SYRIA

PLO

JORDAN

ISRAEL

EGYPT

OMAN

IRAQ

TURKISH AIRBORNE COMMANDO

In 1949, an American paratrooper officer and several NCOs were sent to the Cankiri Infantry School in Turkey with their mission to train a handful of Turkish officers. After qualifying, the Turks were sent to the United States to obtain their instructor ratings and, for several years, were responsible for the training of the first intakes of Turkish paratroopers. After obtaining their 'jump wings', the first locally-trained paratroopers were integrated with the 1st Airborne Platoon of the Guard Regiment. In 1958, the second airborne platoon was formed. As part of their commitment to NATO, US forces landed in Ankara with large quantities of equipment and training capacities. One year later, the 1st Airborne Company was formed, but Turkish High Command was more ambitious and within five years, a three-battalion airborne brigade had been created.

In January 1974, the whole brigade ws heli-lifted or dropped over Cyprus for operation in the Kyrenia region. In no time, the well equipped and highly trained Turkish paras crushed the Greek Cypriot rebellion. For the first time ever, NATO members found themselves on opposite sides during an open conflict. The fighting over, Turkish command assessed the results and, convinced of the efficiency of its airborne forces, decided to supplement Parasütaï Piyade (Airborne brigade) with an additional two para-commando brigades (Parasütaï Komando Piyade). These were entrusted with a wider range of missions, such as opposing the extremist movements that were rife in the 80s, and fighting the Kurd and Armenian guerillas. The airborne brigade was solely tasked with opposing a conventional enemy within the framework of Turkey's commitment to NATO.

Each brigade (airborne and para-commando) comprises 5,000 men distributed among three battalions and support companies. The airborne brigade has its own artillery company.

Made-up of career soldiers and conscripts, Turkish airborne units have earned a fearsome reputation for harsh training and high combativity. Currently, Turkey is rallying support from NATO countries to update the equipment of its defence forces.

The Turkish Air Force has an airborne battalion known as 'search and rescue unit'. Created in 1962 in Ankara, this unit has been progressively beefed up to have detachments posted all over the Turkish territory.

The Turkish Navy also has a sizeable combat divers and pocket submarine force whose members are all parachute qualified.

Above.
In 1991 in Kurdistan, an NCO from the Para-commando brigade recce unit. A qualified free-faller, this highly trained para-commando is fighting the PPK Kurds opposed to Ankara. He wears the airborne camouflage outfit and a tactical vest. He is armed with an HK MP-5 and two hand grenades.

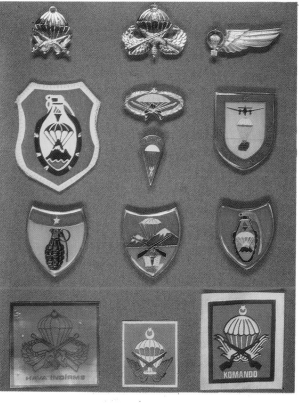

Right.
Various Turkish airborne and para-commando badges: From left to right and from top to bottom: Airborne qualification badge, para-commando qualification badge, 1st Para-Commando Brigade sleeve insignia, para-commando qualification badge, pre-military airborne badge, airborne transport badge, 2nd Para-commando Brigade chest badge, commando school badge, 1st Para-commando brigade chest insignia, combat dress airborne qualification badge, other version of the airborne qualification badge, cloth combat dress cloth airborne qualification badge.

A Syrian para-commando in the Saudi desert during the 1989-90 Gulf War.

84

SYRIAN PARA -COMMANDO

Continuing antagonism towards Israel has dominated the last three and a half decades of Syrian history. In 1958 Damascus decided to boost the efficiency of its armed forces by raising an airborne company. Expanded into a battalion one year later, the unit was dispatched to Egypt as part of a joint Egyptian-Syrian brigade. Following the dissolution ot the United Arab Republic, the paras were repatriated in 1960 and formed the cadre for several commando battalions. Armed and advised by the Soviets, the Syrians adopted Red Army tactics and, unlike western armies, were trained to operate in massive formations or as shock troops.

In the 1960s, the Syrians made numerous raids into Israeli territory where they ambushed convoys with rocket launchers.

Oddly, the Syrian paras were not deployed during the Six-Day War but intervened in the Yom Kippur War when a mixed unit (composed of elements from 82nd Para Battalion and 1st Commando Group) captured Mount Hermon in the Golan Heights after savage hand-to-hand fighting. It took Israeli paras several days to wrest the position back from the Syrians.

The Syrian Army was reshuffled shortly after the war, which did not stop Syrian SFs from raiding Israeli positions on the Golan Heights. In 1976, Syria intervened in Lebanon and during an engagement at Shtura, the commandos were pitted against a new foe: the Palestinians. In 1986, the battalion was increased to brigade strength while over 30 commando battalions (known as *al-Wahdat al-Kassa* or special forces) were raised. Of that number, 10 were based in the Beka'a Valley, Lebanon, and answered to the Special Forces Brigade. Para-Commandos were always in the thick of the action and in February 1982, one of their battalions was integrated within a 1,7000-man force mustered to capture the city of Hama. The battle raged for 10 days, and when the city eventually fell, 25,000 of its inhabitants had been killed.

When the Israelis intervened in Lebanon later that same year, Syrian commandos were dispatched to Jessine and covered the withdrawal of Syria's 1st Armoured Division. They managed to slow down Tsahal columns through a series of ambushes and, later, a Syrian airborne battalion held back the Israelis attacking the mountain town of Ein-Zakhlata.

Syria is thought to have reduced the number of its SF units and today probably fields about 10 para and 20 commando battalions consolidated within the Special Forces Division. Most Syrian commandos are volunteers, totally devoted to President Assad, and required to belong to the Alawite sect to ensure loyalty.

Other SF units are the 'Defence Companies' (*Saraya ad-Difa* or Defenders of the Regime) generally airborne trained and used in the commando role. They too are Alawite and provide Assad's personal guard (unofficially, the defence companies are commanded by the president's brother).

Syrian Para-Commando badges and insignia. From left to right and from top to bottom: current airborne qualification badge; early model (introduced in the 1960s); basic badge variant. Bottom: 1st Class badge variant. Left: airborne shoulder patch. Right: Commando insignia.

A Syrian para NCO of 15th Airborne Battalion during a mission in Lebanon in 1981. As often with elite forces, the soldier's attire is somewhat casual and combines the maroon beret sporting the eagle of the Syrian Republic with a jumper of British Army origin. His camouflage trousers are a copy of the Pakistani model while the blue patch of airborne forces together with the blue lanyard of the Ba'as party are worn on the right shoulder. He is armed with a folding-butt AKM (airborne version of the AK-47) and carries the spare magazines in a chest webbing. Secondary armament includes a Czech-made CZ-75 9mm handgun.

85

PALESTINIAN COMMANDO

In 1948, the creation of the state of Israel forced hundreds of thousands of Palestinians to flee their homeland and seek shelter in neighbouring Arab countries. These settlements became the crucible of Palestinian resistance forces. Over the years, described as 'terrorists' by the Israelis and known as 'freedom fighters' to their Arab brethren, the Palestinians have set-up a multiplicity of underground organisations, and more recently a regular army known as the Palestine Liberation Army has appeared. The constant reshuffle of Palestinian forces makes it difficult to accurately trace the history of each specific formation, but Palestinian special units can be readily distinguished from the regular forces.

In the early sixties, Egyptian President Nasser decided to create three Palestinian brigades. They were deployed between Egypt, Syria and Lebanon. In 1967, they took part in the war on the Arab side but, as the result of their unpreparedness, performed badly. The following year, Yasser Arafat's PLO chose Beirut as its 'capital city'. Meanwhile, no fewer then 11 factions had appeared, and started to create reliable military units capable of taking on the Israelis. However, in September 1970 (later known as Black September), the Palestinians suffered their first major defeat when the armies of Jordan's King Hussein chased them out towards Lebanon after much bitter fighting.

As the Palestinian factions were getting stronger, the three PLA brigades were integrated with the Syrian army. In 1975, civil war broke out in Lebanon. One of its causes was the massive presence of Palestinians in that country. In the early stages, Syria came to their rescue by sending-in PLA units backed-up by 5 battalions (roughly 1,000 men) levied from AS-Sa'iga(Thunder), a Syrian-trained, superbly equipped Palestinian formation.

With Arab cash flowing in, the PLO was then at the height of its power and weapons arrived in large quantities. Consequently, the Palestinian Revolution Council decided to set up several special units, among them Force 17 and Force 14. The size of a battalion, Force 17 was made up of the best elements selected from the other factions. Originally, its officers were trained in East Germany. From then on, and until 1985, East German instructors trained recruits in Syria and Lebanon.

Thorough and harsh training gave the PLO a crack unit, skilled in hand-to-hand fighting, parachuting, combat diving, signalling and survival techniques. Chemical warfare training was received in Czechoslovakia (members of this unit are Yasser Arafat's personal bodyguards). Force 14 was granted its own air capacity and until 1988 operated twenty combat and transport aircraft, (Mig 21, Fokker F-28, Alouette III) all based in Yemen. Its pilots were trained in Romania and Yugoslavia. Meanwhile, the other Palestinian factions had grown and in 1980, they had reached significant strength. The Syrian-based Popular Front for the Liberation of Palestine comprised five infantry battalions and one artillery battalion; the Democratic Front for the Liberation of Palestine fielded 1,000 Syrian-trained men; the Popular Front for the Liberation of Palestine had a Commanding General with an 800-men strong battalion including a special combat diver unit trained in the DDR or the Soviet Union; and the Front for the Liberation of Palestine could muster 300 highly specialised men, trained to carry out attacks on Israel with unorthodox means such as balloons, gliders or ULM.

1982 saw the end of massive Palestinian presence in Lebanon. In June, the Israelis launched operation Litani, aimed at suppressing once and for all the Palestinian threat. 15,000 strong, the Palestinians were no match for Tsahal (the Israeli army) and even the OLP special units were successively beaten. In mid-June, a ceasefire agreement was reached and the survivors of Force 17 left Beirut by sea never to return. Today even though several Palestinian fighting formations have returned to Lebanon, their power has been considerably reduced. The remainder are now quartered in Tunisia, Libya, Syria, Iraq and Yemen.

Right, top to bottom.
Three rare versions of PLO Commando metal badges worn in the seventies and later replaced by a raised metal model inspired by Syrian Special Forces.

The illustration depicts a Palestinian Force 17 member in Beirut's southern suburbs in 1982. Wearing a Korean-made camouflage outfit, he carries the Palestinian standard equipment reduced to a minimum to facilitate movements among ruins and obstacles. He is armed with the most unusual VZ-52 assault rifle, Czech-made version of the Soviet AK-47 with the early night-vision sight. Extremely efficient in steet fighting, this weapon is fitted with its specific bayonet. The armament is completed by a powerful 7.65mm Skorpion and two Soviet-made defensive hand grenades.

JORDANIAN SPECIAL FORCES

Albeit a small force, Jordan's Army has always been regarded as one of the best-trained in the Arab world, and the same applies to its special forces. Totalling 70,000 men, most of them Bedouins loyal to the Hashemite dynasty, the elite of this top notch army is the 101st SF Brigade.

A British-trained airborne company (Special Service Group) was raised in 1963 and later expanded into King Hussein's personal guard. Deployed alongside the Arab Legion in Cisjordania during the Six-Day War, the para-commandos defended Jerusalem with tooth and nail from Tsahal paras. On 30 June 1969, the Special Service Group was converted into the SF *'Saiqua'* (storm) Brigade and one year later, these forces played a decisive role when the Palestinians were ousted from Jordan.

This episode gave Hussein's para-commandos (based near the Basnam Palace) the opportunity to demonstrate their loyalty to the ruler.

When Jordan became the target of Palestinian extremists, the Brigade improved its anti-terrorist techniques and in 1976, a group took part in the liberation of hostages detained at a hotel in Amman.

One of the Brigade's four battalions was based in Oman on a permanent basis financed by the King. This unit also provided commando and airborne tuition to trainees from other services.

The Brigade is now reduced to three 500-man battalions, organised into three-platoon companies, and equipped in the same way as standard light infantry units (anti-tank and air defence weapons, recoilless guns, Dragoon and Stinger rocket launchers) and issued with 4 x 4 Land Rover light vehicles. Also on strength is a free-faller team specialising in deep recce and sabotage. Hailing for the larger part from Bedouin tribes, most SF recruits are volunteers, in top physical shape and are only selected after stringent tests. Basic training lasts six months and is followed by more specialised coaching in close combat, recce, demolition and airborne techniques (all SF personnel are parachute qualified). Regularly, Jordanian SFs take part in joint manoeuvres with US Special Forces and British SAS. The Brigade is regarded as one of the best in the Middle East.

A Jordanian commando of the 'Saiqua' Brigade pictured in September 1970 during the battle of Amman against the Palestinians. Although the unit's name has changed (it used to be known as Special Service Group), the man's kit is unaltered and includes a faithful copy of the British Denison smock worn with a mixture of British 37 Pattern and US equipment (trousers and boots). The commando is armed with a US M-2 carbine fitted with a 30-round magazine and scope. The checked headgear is the traditional red and white 'kefiyeh' adorned with the Jordanian Army badge. Special forces have maroon berets and wear US steel helmets in combat.

Jordanian current airborne qualification badges. From top to bottom: senior badge (awarded for 30 jumps); basic badge; cloth patch topped with the royal crown.

87

ISRAELI PARA

The Israeli *'Tzahan'* (Hebrew for paratrooper) enjoys unrivalled popularity among his countrymen, outshining all the other remarkable IDF units defending the Jewish state. Actively involved in all the struggles Israel had to face since coming into being, Israeli paras have fought with distinction on every front.

Raised in 1948, during the war between Jewish settlers, the Arabs and the British, Israel's first airborne unit consisted of a mixed bag of British-trained veterans who had seen action with SOE, Palm'ach graduates of a parachute course held in Czechoslovakia, former resistance fighters, ghetto survivors and a handful of adventurers. These men were sent straight into battle after a sketchy refresher course and several jumps.

In 1961, Moshe Dayan decided to amalgamate the airborne battalion with the famous 101 Unit, a force specialising in reprisal operations. The newly created force was known as 102 Unit and served as a cadre for the training of future Israeli paratroops. In 1954-55 the paratroops were expanded to brigade strength.

During the 1956 Sinai Campaign, 1st Battalion of 102 Airborne Brigade was dropped on the Mitla Pass in a very successful operation which ended in defeat for the Egyptians. One year later, Tsahal raised one additional and one reserve airborne brigade.

During the Six-Day War, the paras struck at the Syrian borders and seized the Golan Heights but their greatest moment came on 7 June 1967 when they recaptured the Old City of Jerusalem. More than half of the Arab Legion elite soldiers defending the town were killed in that action.

From 1968 to 1973, the paras undertook more raids against the Palestinians, including those against the PLO headquarters in Jordan (21 March 1968, 250 enemy killed), the destruction of numerous Arab aircraft at Beirut Airport (12 December 1968), and the capture and return from Egypt to Israel of a complete Soviet radar installation (23 December 1969).

In 1973, the Yom Kippur War broke out. After recovering from their initial setback, the Israelis soon regained the upper hand with 31st Brigade fighting on the Golan Heights while the other brigade crossed the Suez Canal into Egyptian home territory. The paras were victorious again although they had not been deployed in their airborne role.

On 3 July 1976, four C-130 Hercules transport aircraft carrying 'red berets' took off from Israel and headed for Uganda, some 5,000km away, to liberate the passengers and crew of a hijacked Air France A-300 detained in Entebbe by 'Field Marshal' Amin Dada's soldiers. Mounted at short notice, Operation 'Jonathan' was a brilliant success marred only by the deaths of the paras' commanding officer and four hostages. In 1982, Israeli paras riding APCs crammed to the brim thrust into Lebanon during Operation 'Peace in Galilee' which turned out to be a military success but a political failure.

Young Israelis are conscripted for three years (two for women) and paras are exclusively recruited from volunteers. Training is stringent and arduous, with the emphasis being placed on weaponry, sabotage heliborne assaults and night combat (raiding an enemy camp - Palestinian or other - constitutes an excellent 'peacetime' baptism of fire). 'Wings' are awarded after three day and two night jumps. Currently, Israel fields five airborne brigades (two of these are at or very near full strength; one is above 50 per cent and two are at cadre strength).

August 1982. An Israeli para waits for orders during a mission in the suburbs of Beirut. Kitted out like all other IDF members, he wears a Kevlar splinter-proof vest over his 1981 Model olive green fatigues. He has been issued with the latest webbing with integrated pouches holding 12 M-16, AK-47 or Galil spare magazines. Smaller than most models, the lightweight helmet affords good protection. He is armed with a folding-butt, short-barrelled 5.56mm Galil assault rifle replacing the UZI submachine-gun that remained on issue for 20 years. The transceiver he carries on his back is the Israeli-made version of the US AN/RPC-25 model.

Isreali airborne qualification badges. From left to right and from top to bottom: Jumpmaster badge (awarded for 50 jumps); standard airborne badge (green background for the jumpaster version); Para-Commando badge; parachute packer badge.

ISRAELI NAVY COMMANDO

Israel's Navy Commandos trace their roots back to 1943 when Jewish Defence Forces in Palestine created Pal'Yam (Naval Companies) with fighters recruited from fishing villages. Specialising in clandestine landings and sabotage action, the members of these units assisted the Allies during World War 2. In 1948, the Pal'Yams evolved into Heyl Hayam (Israeli Navy) and spawned the Kommando Yami (marine commandos) as the war of independence was in full swing. Although their numbers were scant and their means limited, the Kommando Yami carried out several spectacular operations against Arab shipping.

Regarded as the elite of the fledgling state's forces, the commandos fulfilled hundreds of missions against objectives in Egypt, Syria and Lebanon. A combat diver unit numbering some 20 men evolved from the Naval Companies and trained in France at the St Mandrier Combat Diver School. The Israeli Navy commandos made their first 'official' appearance when, on 5 June 1967 at 9pm, six of them were captured near Alexandria in Egypt after being delivered there by the submarine INS *Tanin*. This fiasco resulted from the Israelis' reluctance to stick to the approach tactics they had been taught as well as a gross underestimation of their Arab adversaries.

Navy commandos had a busy time in the war of attrition that followed the Six-Day War. Two of the commandos' most famous operations took place in summer 1969. On 21 June, they raided the base of Ras El-Abadi destroying the Egyptian air defences there. On 19 July, they struck again when they captured Green Island which commands the southern approaches of the Suez Canal. Regarded as impregnable, the site fell to the Israelis after a pitched battle that raged for three hours. A more discreet attack was made on 7 September by combat divers who sank two torpedo launches in Ras Sabat harbour. Several commandos were killed, however, while removing charges from Israeli ships in Eilat harbour.

On the night of 16-17 October, four divers made their way through the underwater net protecting Port Said, and one pair fixed charges to two Egyptian landing craft, whilst the second team vanished without trace.

On 9, 11, 18, 21 and 22 October, the commandos attacked A'Ardaqua naval base and, on 7 June 1982, took part in the largest amphibious operation ever carried out by the Israeli army when they landed north of Sidon in Lebanon during Operation 'Peace for Galilee'. More recently (April 1988), a 30-man commando made up of men from Mossad (Israeli Intelligence Service) and Kommando Yami landed in Tunisia to eliminate Abou Jihad, the PLO's second in command.

All Kommando Yami are volunteers selected after a battery of arduous medical, psychological and physical tests which weed out about 70% of the applicants. The remaining 30% then undertake an 18-month training course and qualify as paras, commandos, free-fallers and some as combat divers. Occasionally a few commandos may be called on to operate abroad and train in intelligence work. Currently, Israel fields one Kommando Yami unit and a 20 men combat diver outfit. ❑

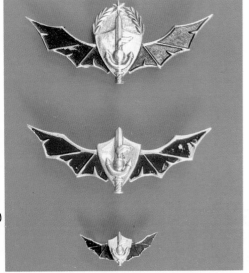

A member of Kommando Yami commissioned with the combat diver unit. The man is shown in Lebanon, in June 1982. Clad in a black neoprene diver suit, the marine commando has discarded his Oxygers aqualung and hooked up his fins on his assault webbing (known as Ephod) before a recce mission. The Israeli is armed with an AKM assault rifle with two taped magazines.

Several Israeli Marine Commando badges. From top to bottom: master qualification badge; basic qualification badge (nicknamed Kanfei Ataleif or bat's ears); lapel insignia for civilian suit. The badges are worn above the left breast pocket.

EGYPTIAN PARA

Raised after an Egyptian military attaché visited Britain's airborne school at Ringway in 1946, the Egyptian airborne forces are the oldest in the Arab world. However, several years elapsed before four officers were parachute-trained in Britain. They were soon followed by several NCOs who received maintenance, packing and jump tuition. On 10 July 1952, the first batch graduated and made its first mass jump near Cairo. Only 12 days later, the Egyptian parachute school was officially created. Originally answering to the air force, the school was later placed under army control. In 1956, two officers were sent to the USA to attend the free-fall and airdrop courses, and by September Egypt had commissioned three airborne companies to form the 1st Airborne Battalion. Four years later, the force was expanded into a Brigade and, for a short while, included a Syrian airborne battalion.

In the early 1960s, the Egyptian government decided to follow a different political course and airborne training was entrusted to Egypt's new friends, the Soviets, who introduced their own parachutes and equipment. In 1960, Para battalion 'El Sheitan' (the devil) was deployed in the Congo with the UN Blue Helmets. In September, several airborne companies were dropped over Latakia in Syria but failed to seize the harbour. In 1962, 'El Sheitan' Battalion was reintegrated with the rest of the Brigade in Yemen and fought for five years against royalist supporters. In this war, Egyptian paras made several operational jumps against the opponents to Sanaa's government.

From 1969, paras and commandos conducted numerous raids across the Suez Canal against the Israelis entrenched in the Bar-Lev Line. In 1971, Cairo dispatched an airborne battalion to Sudan when Khartoum's government needed assistance to crush a rebellion.

During the 1973 Yom Kippur War, paras were intensively involved and even won their foes' admiration. Under the energetic leadership of General Shaazli, the 'father' of Egyptian airborne forces, Egypt had created two airborne brigades (140th and 182nd) and these forces were heli-transported or landed in the Sinai. When the Israeli counter-attacked, the 140th Airborne Brigade was involved in bitter hand-to-hand fighting against its counterparts of the Israeli 247th Airborne Brigade.

According to some sources, Egyptian paras were dropped in Lybia in 1977 to put paid to Colonel Ghadaffi's expansionist ambitions.

Currently, Egypt fields two airborne brigades and 26 commando battalions (the latter organised and tasked with different missions). Most Egyptian paras are volunteers who train at the Ashmun Parachute School near Cairo. Ranking alongside commandos and combat divers as the elite of Egyptian forces, Egyptian paras also train the airborne forces of other Arab countries, such as such as the Yemen and Sudan. ❒

An Egyptian para of the 140th Airborne brigade pictured during Exercise 'Bright Star' in 1986. Egyptian airborne commandos and paras are issued with a reversible combat uniform: its spotted pattern is shown here, the other side is for desert fighting conditions. Although American assistance had by then superseded Soviet military aid, the para's equipment is still Warsaw Pact issue: magazine pouches for East German-made AK-74, helmet with cloth cover and Soviet 7.62mm x 39 assault rifle.

From top to bottom and from left to right: 4th Class airborne qualification badge; 3rd Class airborne qualification badge; instructor badge; shoulder badge; Number One suit badge.

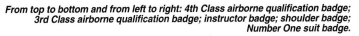

Egyptian para-commando pictured in the Saudi desert a short distance away from Iraqi front line positions. These elite soldiers made up the spearhead of Egyptian forces in the Gulf.

EGYPTIAN COMMANDO

In the 1960s, the arrival of the first Soviet advisors in Egypt prompted Egyptian High Command to create commando units. Using the same combat tactics as the airborne companies created in 1953 - and which were extended into an airborne brigade in 1957 - within a few months the Egyptian 'cadre' and the Soviet advisors had trained enough volunteers to form a company. In 1963, a commando detachment, amounting roughly to two companies, was sent to the Yemen to oppose the Saudi-backed royalists. Until 1967, the commandos carried out all their operations alongside paras, their major task being to protect the Egyptian expeditionary force HQ and to act as bodyguards for high ranking officers. Before being sent out to this theatre of operations, most commandos had been parachute-trained. When the Six-Day War broke out, the Egyptian government was compelled to recall first the elite forces, and then its whole expeditionary force. No operational report makes any mention of actions conducted by Egyptian commandos against Israeli forces. In 1969, Egyptian command decided to launch special operations behind Israeli lines, and commandos executed sabotage missions and incursions beyond the Bar-Lev line on the Suez Canal. In 1971, fighting alongside a para battalion, half a commando company was sent to Sudan to help the Khartoum government suppress an all-out insurrection.

In 1972, Egyptian armed forces fielded some 28 commando battalions. These were distributed into two commando brigades mustering 1,000 men each, and organised into four reduced battalions. These brigades answered exclusively to 'As-Saiqa' (thunderbolt), a command grouping all special forces. Two years later, the Yom Kippur War broke out when Arab countries took the initiative and attacked Israel. Egyptian commandos were at the spearhead, operating on the Suez Canal where they breached Israeli lines, or were helo-transported to the Sinai where they set up anti-tank blockades to hold off Israeli counterthrusts. The first days of fighting were crowned with success: by destroying dozens of enemy tanks and aircraft, the Egyptian commandos avenged the humiliation suffered in the Six-Day war. In spite of their gallantry however, they were overwhelmed and forced to give in to the Israelis' superior tactical skills. But even when outflanked, hardly any one of them were captured.

In 1977 and 1978, the commandos operated in Libya, and their missions were reminiscent of those carried out in World War Two by the British Long Range Desert Group. They destroyed Ghadafi's armoured concentrations and put paid to his plans to invade Egypt. Representing the Arab forces in Saudi Arabia during Operation Desert Storm, the Egyptian Army only deployed the equivalent of a commando brigade. Egyptian intervention during the attack on Kuwait was low key, with Egyptian commandos clearing paths through minefields for the full deployment of allied forces.

Currently, the Egyptian army fields two brigades. Quartered around Cairo, their establishment is equally split between conscripts and career soldiers who provide the cadre, the teams tasked with special anti-terrorist duties, and the deep recce divers.

Unlike the paras who are kept as strategic reserve, the commandos are used for shock missions such as breaching through the front line, anti-tank warfare and secret missions in enemy territory.   ❏

Various insignia and qualifcation badges awarded to Egyptian commandos :
From top to bottom and from left to right:
Commando badge (reduced size) worn on walking-out dress. Commando badge and title worn on the left shoulder. Combat diver qualification badge. 3rd Class airborne qualification badge. 4th Class airborne qualification badge.

Egyptian commando belonging to 1st Commando Brigade, shown in 1985 in the vicinity of Cairo during a joint exercise with paras of the US 82nd Airborne. The man wears the reversible camouflage outfit, depicted here in its 'sand pattern', a garment identical to the model worn in the 1970s by Egyptian paras and Palestinian units.
The commando is armed with a Soviet-made LPO-50 flame thrower which his standard issue to all ex Warsaw Pact forces. Weighing 15kg (empty) and 23kg (full), this weapon has a maximum range of 50 to 70 metres. The man's airborne qualification badge is particularly noteworthy.

OMANI SPECIAL FORCES

Located on the tip of the Arabian peninsula - a position of crucial strategic importance - the Sultanate of Oman has always enjoyed a privileged relationship with Great Britain and currently, more than 1,000 British officers and NCOs are serving as instructors in the ranks of the Sultanate's army.

When the south of the country was torn by revolt in 1965, Britain supplied massive aid to Oman and dispatched SAS units to check enemy infiltration (assistance was also provided by Iranian and Jordanian special forces) and more British elite units were dispatched to Oman when the fighting peaked in 1970.

The Sultanate's crying need for specialised forces was keenly felt in these times of crisis and in October 1974, on a decision of Sultan Qaboos Bin Said, volunteers from the Oman Gendarmerie were trained in parachuting in Saudi Arabia and in 1975 formed into the company-sized D (Parachute) Squadron. A further two courses were organised in early 1976 and January 1977.

Wishing to restore peace along its southern border, Saudi Arabia financed the establishment of an airborne school in Oman. Selected from among the best, six Omani paras obtained their instructor ratings in Saudi Arabia and later provided the cadre for Oman's Parachute Training School in 1977. By June 1980, an 180-man squadron had been trained at the Rustaq Parachute School (which remains an organic part of D Squadron) and designated the Oman Parachute Squadron. In addition to the paras, the Squadron has several free-faller teams specialising in sabotage and deep recce.

Besides the army, navy and air force, (a total of 21,500 volunteers), Oman has another armed force, the Sultan's Royal Household, answering exclusively to the Sultan and composed of the Royal Guards Brigade, Royal Yacht, Royal Flight and the Sultan's Special Forces. The Sultan's SF is a 400-man battalion-sized unit, SAS-advised and recruited exclusively from among the inhabitants of the Dhofar area, once notorious for its rebellious activities. They are trained in SAS skills including LRRP, small boat handling and long-range desert motorised operations. ❏

Omani insignia and badges. From top to bottom and left to right: Cap badge (airborne model); basic airborne qualification badge (army personnel); standard airborne qualification badge; combat uniform Special Forces patch; Special Forces parade dress embroidered patch.

An officer commissioned with the Sultanate of Oman's special forces, a unit operating as a Para-Commando battalion and answering directly to the Sultan. Clad in a desert pattern camouflage outfit, the man is equipped with US webbing and armed with the superlative Steyr AUG HBAR-T 5.56mm assault rifle, shown here in its light machine-gun version (heavy barrel and bipod). The weapon is fitted with a night vision Startron sniper scope fixed to the carrying handle.

IRAQI COMMANDO

In 1942, more than 150 Iraqi volunteers - officers and NCOs - were airborne trained at Habbaniya Airport by British paras of 156th Battalion (in those days, Iraq had been granted semi-independent status by Britain). These men were gathered into an airborne company and attached to the British 11th Parachute Battalion. Dispatched to Italy in August 1943, the Iraqi unit fought as ground troops near the Aegean Sea but disbanded six months later.

Meanwhile, more Iraqis were trained and by 1948, 350 had graduated. About 200 of them were deployed against the Israelis and defended successfully the fortress of Jessin for two days. Their achievements however, did not result in the creation of airborne forces, as after training Iraqi paras were returned individually to their units.

From 1954 to 1958, Iraqis were regularly sent to Britain for training and the first batch graduated there on 7 April. In July 1958, the first locally-trained airborne unit was commissioned. An independent company had been raised in the meantime and expanded four years later into a battalion.

After the 1964 agreements with the United States, members of US 3rd SFG set up a commando school in Iraq (which didn't prevent Baghdad from secretly having paras receiving commando training from the Egyptians in a Sinai camp).

In May 1965, the 'Saikes' (commandos) were commissioned into the 1st Commando Battalion, followed two years later by the 2nd Commando Battalion. In December 1969, both units were mustered into the 17th Independent Airborne Brigade (commandos and paras train at the same school).

The elite of Iraqi forces, these units were regularly dispatched to the north of the country and deployed against the Kurds. During the 1973 Yom Kippur War, the Brigade fought in Syria and was opposed to Israeli armour at Tel Antar on the Golan Heights. In 1975, when war broke out in Lebanon, 'volunteers' fought on the Muslim side while Iraqi instructors coached Palestinian and Eretrean cadres in commando techniques. In September 1980, Iraqi paras and commandos spearheaded the attack against Iran. They displayed their courage in the defence and recapture of a marshy area in the Basrah region. During that conflict, the SF brigade made an operational jump over the island of Majnun to cut Iranian communication lines. During the eight-year war, the commando units expanded ito seven SF brigades, each attached to an army corps.

Along with the Airborne Brigade and the Mountain Division, Iraqi commando units constitute the general reserve while the Republican Guard , itself an elite corps, also has its own SF division, the 99th. During the Gulf War, these units manned defensive positions around Kuwait. ❑

Basrah, 1988. An Iraqi Commando corporal of the 1st SF Brigade. Equipped like conventional Iraqi forces, nothing but his camouflage uniform indicates that he belongs to an elite unit. He has two ammo pouches and is armed with the famous folding-butt AK-47 assault rifle. Commandos never wear webbing and are often issued with canvas shoes.

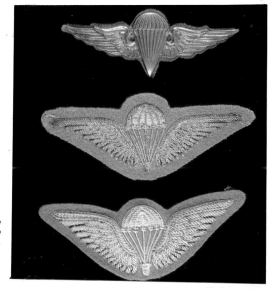

Iraqi parachute qualification badges. From top to bottom: basic badge; parade dress badge; early airborne patch issued in the 1960s (but still worn by some officers).

ASIA, AUSTRALASIA

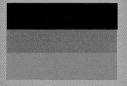 AFGHANISTAN

 PAKISTAN

 SRI-LANKA

 INDIA

THAILAND

 INDONESIA

SOUTH VIETNAM

KOREA

CHINA

JAPAN

AUSTRALIA

NEW ZEALAND

97

AFGHAN PARA-COMMANDO

Aware of the Soviet threat and wishing to placate his American allies, in the late 1960s Afghan King Zaher Khan decided to update his armed forces and form Para-Commando units. Washington was only waiting for this opportunity to dispatch several members of its Special Forces to train the future Afghan commando brigades. In 1973 however, the King was overthrown in a coup instigated by Afghan communists (acting on the Kremlin's advice) and the ranks of the armed forces were purged of all royalist supporters. Thus, a crippling blow had been dealt to Afghan Special Forces from which they had hardly recovered by 1978. One year later, scores of Red Army instructors arrived in Afghanistan to take over command of Kabul's armed forces and during the December 1979 invasion, several Soviet-led Afghan commandos contributed to the seizure of major cities by the Red Army.

After the invasion, the Afghan commando force quickly expanded and soon amounted to two brigades, the 444th and 666th, both based in Kabul. One year later, another two were created when the 37th, also based in the capital city, and the 38th quartered at Parwan, were commissioned. Meanwhile, unrest was sweeping through the ranks of the Afghan Army and the 26th Independent Airborne Battalion mutineed only to be crushed by Red Army tanks after several days of fighting. Wiser after this experience, the Soviets endeavoured to foster the commandos' loyalty to the regime through tighter recruiting and more politically-minded leadership. By 1981, the commando brigades were regarded as the only reliable Afghan force and extensively used alongside their Soviet counterparts in major operations.

Protracted fighting however, had cut bloody swathes in the commandos' ranks and to keep losses down, Kabul and Soviet High Command decided to resort to new tactics and reorganised the force into smaller, more flexible units. During the war, the commandos made several operational jumps and intervened near the Pakistani border to try and cut the resistance's supply lines. The commandos fought on until the 1988 Soviet withdrawal, operating mostly in small parties infiltrated into Mujaheedin-held territories. Their successes however, were scant and they could never totally wrest from the guerillas the control of the mountains.

Currently, all commando units and conventional armed forces have been gathered into major cities to defend them from the insurgents. Officially, only volunteers were recruited for service with the Para-Commandos but it has been established that about 90% of them were dragooned into the force on account of their political reliability. All the officers were trained in the former Soviet Union and have attended specialised courses in military academies and at the Ryazan Higher Airborne Command School near Moscow.

Each brigade has a theoretical strength of 2,000 men, organised into three combat battalions and fielding approximately 550 commandos each. With the exception of Kabul-based units issued with BTR-60 and BTR-70 armoured vehicles, Afghan commandos are almost completely without heavy equipment: 82mm mortars and 14.5mm machine-guns are the heaviest weapons in their arsenal. ❒

From top to bottom. Afghan commando metal qualification badges. First class badge (equivalent to jumpmaster); second class badge awarded after several dozen jumps; third class badge awarded (among others) for a jump in wartime. Interestingly, badges have remained unchanged since the days of the Royal Army.

1985: a member of 37th Para-Commando Brigade, pictured in Kabul during a parade, and clad in a Bulgarian-made camouflage outfit with third-class cloth badge on his chest. In combat however, Afghan commandos used to wear the olive green fatigues on standard issue to Afghan forces with a combat cap replacing the maroon beret. With canvas ammo pouches and AK bayonet dangling from the belt, the Para-Commando is armed with the ubiquitous AKM, the folding butt version of the famous Soviet AK-47.

PAKISTANI NAVY COMMANDO

Pakistan's Naval Special Service Group (referred to as NSSG or SSGN) was created in 1966 when about 100 navy officers were selected and sent to the three SSG (Special Service Groups) training bases run by the Pakistani armed forces at Cherat, Karachi and Peshawar. During the following eight months, the trainees received special forces and commando training, and became thoroughly proficient in all aspects of their new trade (from counter-insurgency tactics and anti-terrorist action to fighting Indian units in the Himalayas). They also qualified as paratroopers and combat divers. One year later, NSSG was created and tasked with special interventions along the coast and in Pakistani territorial waters.

Later, Pakistani high command entrusted NSSG combat divers with the security of the inland waterways in eastern and western Pakistan (today's Bangladesh).

Shortly before western Pakistan was invaded by the Indian army, SSG and NSSG parties raided Bengali rebel camps, but were decimated when opposed to Indian forces. For several days, NSSG units fought at Chittagong while temporarily attached to a marine battalion. To avoid capture, some NSSG members covertly crossed the border into Burma and were repatriated much later.

Currently, NSSG is based in Karachi and answers to Pakistani Navy Command. Subdivided into 10-men platoons, NSSG has the size of a company and executes special missions such as harbour raiding, sabotage and anti-terrorist warfare on behalf of the navy. In wartime, NSSG would operate midget submarines. Parachute training is still conducted at Peshawar airborne school, but the commando and combat diver courses are run at the NSSG naval base in Karachi.

In the 70s, Pakistani navy commandos conducted joint exercises with their Iranian counterparts and US Navy SEALS.

NSSG is also responsible for training Omani and Saudi commandos.

Bottom. From left to right and top to bottom:
**NSSG commando beret metal badge. NSSG training cadre cloth badge.
Combat diver first class shoulder badge. Standard navy cloth badge.**

Left.
Seen in 1991 in the vicinity of Karachi, a Pakistani NSSG commando from one of the anti-terrorist platoons. Members of that unit are clad in the light blue standard Pakistani Navy issue fatigues. The individual load carrying equipment is a locally-made variant of the British 58 Pattern Web Equipment, and the man is armed with a 9mm HK MP-5K submachine gun. The Combat Diver qualification badge is worn on the right sleeve.

SRI LANKAN PARA COMMANDO

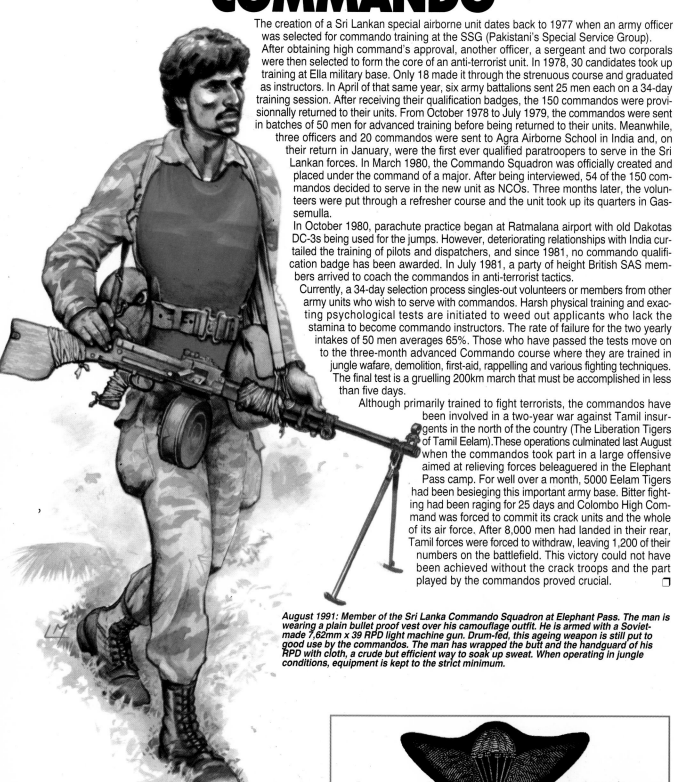

The creation of a Sri Lankan special airborne unit dates back to 1977 when an army officer was selected for commando training at the SSG (Pakistani's Special Service Group). After obtaining high command's approval, another officer, a sergeant and two corporals were then selected to form the core of an anti-terrorist unit. In 1978, 30 candidates took up training at Ella military base. Only 18 made it through the strenuous course and graduated as instructors. In April of that same year, six army battalions sent 25 men each on a 34-day training session. After receiving their qualification badges, the 150 commandos were provisionnally returned to their units. From October 1978 to July 1979, the commandos were sent in batches of 50 men for advanced training before being returned to their units. Meanwhile, three officers and 20 commandos were sent to Agra Airborne School in India and, on their return in January, were the first ever qualified paratroopers to serve in the Sri Lankan forces. In March 1980, the Commando Squadron was officially created and placed under the command of a major. After being interviewed, 54 of the 150 commandos decided to serve in the new unit as NCOs. Three months later, the volunteers were put through a refresher course and the unit took up its quarters in Gassemulla.

In October 1980, parachute practice began at Ratmalana airport with old Dakotas DC-3s being used for the jumps. However, deteriorating relationships with India curtailed the training of pilots and dispatchers, and since 1981, no commando qualification badge has been awarded. In July 1981, a party of height British SAS members arrived to coach the commandos in anti-terrorist tactics.

Currently, a 34-day selection process singles-out volunteers or members from other army units who wish to serve with commandos. Harsh physical training and exacting psychological tests are initiated to weed out applicants who lack the stamina to become commando instructors. The rate of failure for the two yearly intakes of 50 men averages 65%. Those who have passed the tests move on to the three-month advanced Commando course where they are trained in jungle wafare, demolition, first-aid, rappelling and various fighting techniques. The final test is a gruelling 200km march that must be accomplished in less than five days.

Although primarily trained to fight terrorists, the commandos have been involved in a two-year war against Tamil insurgents in the north of the country (The Liberation Tigers of Tamil Eelam).These operations culminated last August when the commandos took part in a large offensive aimed at relieving forces beleaguered in the Elephant Pass camp. For well over a month, 5000 Eelam Tigers had been besieging this important army base. Bitter fighting had been raging for 25 days and Colombo High Command was forced to commit its crack units and the whole of its air force. After 8,000 men had landed in their rear, Tamil forces were forced to withdraw, leaving 1,200 of their numbers on the battlefield. This victory could not have been achieved without the crack troops and the part played by the commandos proved crucial. ❒

August 1991: Member of the Sri Lanka Commando Squadron at Elephant Pass. The man is wearing a plain bullet proof vest over his camouflage outfit. He is armed with a Soviet-made 7,62mm x 39 RPD light machine gun. Drum-fed, this ageing weapon is still put to good use by the commandos. The man has wrapped the butt and the handguard of his RPD with cloth, a crude but efficient way to soak up sweat. When operating in jungle conditions, equipment is kept to the strict minimum.

Opposite, right.
Various Sri Lanka Special Forces qualification badges and insignia:
From top to bottom, left to right:
Cloth airborne badge, worn on parade dress. Metal commando badge worn above the right chest pocket. Commando cloth insignia, worn on maroon beret. Cloth insignia, worn on the sleeve by qualified airborne personnel commissioned outside to airborne units.

INDIAN PARA

Indian airborne forces rank among the oldest in the world, originating in May 1941 when the 50th Indian Parachute Brigade was raised. In October, this was followed by the creation of the 44th Indian Parachute Brigade comprising 152nd Parachute (Indian), 151st (British) and 153rd (Gurkhas). A parachute school was set up in New Delhi and later transferred to Chaklala. In March 1944, the Brigade was deployed on the Imphal front and involved in bitter fighting against the Japanese.

In 1944, British High Command raised the 44th Indian Airborne Brigade and the Independent Indian Parachute Regiment (1st, 2nd, 3rd and 4th Para Battalions, with 1st composed of Hindus and 4th of Muslims) as well as the 60th Medical Unit and the 44th Division Recce Squadron (Sikh). In 1947, when Pakistan came into being as the result of the partition of India, the Division (meanwhile redesignated 2nd Parachute Division) was shared between the two countries with India retaining 1st Kumaon, 1st Punjab, 3rd Mahratta Light Infantry, 3rd Rajput, 4th Rajputana, 2nd Madras and the 60th Medical Unit. The Chaklala Jump School was also turned over to the new state, and a new one set up at Agra. In the 1950s, the para units were reduced and amalgamated into the 50th Brigade which fought the Pakistanis in Kashmir during the 1947-49 war.

India's airborne medical unit was deployed during the Korean War and made an operational jump with US paras over Munsan. Increasing tension on the Chinese border led to the formation of additional battalions between 1963 and 1965, culminating with the creation of the 51st Parachute Brigade. Both brigades fought in the 1965 Indo-Pakisan War but were deployed only as elite infantry.

In 1967, the 1st Parachute Brigade was deployed on the Tibetan border and later fought guerillas in Assam.

During the 1971 war against Pakistan (in what is now known as Bangladesh), the Indian paras and commandos were heavily committed and captured Jessore before turning on Bangladesh's future capital city, Dacca. On 16 December, that city was taken by the paras of 2nd Para Battalion who had been dropped over Tangaliu. Meanwhile, 9th Para-Commando Battalion thrust into Kashmir and 10th Para-Commando operated successfully in the extreme south on the Indian Ocean shore.

Currently, Indian airborne forces amount to eight parachute battalions organised into two independent brigades (50th and 51st), each with its own training and support units (command, artillery and signals). These battalions are complemented by 9th and 10th Para-Commando, operating independently and fielding three companies each.

Indian paras and para-commandos are volunteers, recruited from among civilian and army personnel, and selected after a 30-day screening process that eliminates about 70% of applicants. Trainees graduate at Arga and obtain their 'wings' and maroon beret after four daytime and one night jump. ❐

1975: a lieutenant commissioned with one of the 51st Parachute Brigade's artillery units. British influence is conspicuous in the famous Denison smock (a new model with slightly different colours has been introduced since), the trousers, holster, and 1937 Pattern webbing pouches. Identical to the British model, the 'wings' are worn on the right shoulder while the rank insignia are displayed on the shoulder tabs. The maroon beret is adorned with the airborne artillery badge (identical to the British model but topped by a five-pointed star). The lieutenant is armed with a Browning GO P35 9mm handgun, weighing 0.860kg and holding 13 rounds.

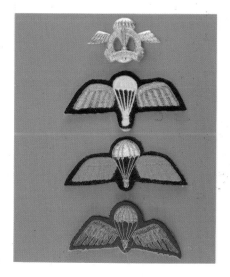

From top to bottom: Indian airborne qualification badges; cap badge; basic qualification cloth patch; summer outfit patch; parade dress badge.

THAI RECON MARINE

In 1965, Thailand's Royal Marine Corps formed a recce company and entrusted it with beach reconnaissance and obstacle clearing.

The unit included combat divers trained to mark out the beaches and hold them until the landing of the main force. Like the US Recon Marines who trained them for several years, the Thais could also carry out special operations behind enemy lines.

Thailand's Marine Corps originated in 1904 when a battalion was raised and specially trained to protect the royal family during its river moves. In 1961, the corps comprised three combat battalions and one command company. As a result of tension with the Khmer Rouge, the second battalion took up position on the Cambodian border, and four years later, the skirmishes had flared up into an all-out war in which the Thai Marines were soon heavily committed. In 1972, several platoons were sent to Laos to fight communist-led Pathet Lao in the Plaine des Jarres. To counter the Vietnamese threat on the Khmer border, Thai headquarters decided to expand the Recon company into a battalion, and the new unit comprised a command company, an amphibious recce company (combat divers), and two motorised amphibious companies. Currently, Thailand's Marine Corps fields 2,000 men organised into six marine regiments, one artillery regiment and three recce and assault battalions known as Recon Marines.

Based at Sattaship Naval Base, Bangkok and Chantabury, the battalions are commanded by a lieutenant colonel. All Recon marines are recruited among the corps and have been selected after a three-month course at the Sattahip Special Warfare Centre.

All are volunteers and are proficient in naval and land warfare tactics. Frequent exercises are carried out on the Cambodian border to add realism to training. All Recon marines are parachute qualified and have logged at least eight jumps (including one at night and one over water).

Presently, Thai command is considering expanding the force into an autonomous division and providing it with its own air support. Thailand has decided to become a sea power and has purchased several large ships, including a light aircraft carrier and assault craft. The rise in power is likely to increase the role of Thailand's Recon marines. ❏

Left.
Thai Recon marine of 3rd Battalion, 2nd Brigade, Royal Marine Corps, pictured in the Chantabury region in 1990. Originally trained by US Recon Marines, the Thai Recons have supplemented their locally-made outfit with the famed cap of the US Marines. The badge of the corps is also identical and includes the globe and the anchor, but with the mother goddess of Thailand replacing the eagle. The equipment of this Recon is identical to his US counterpart, and includes an assault rig with magazine pouches. The weapon is the M-16A1 assault rifle. The marine commando badge is worn on the right of the chest, while the naval-para and battalion insignias are worn on the left.

Right.
**Various Thai badges and qualification badges:
1. Royal Thai Marine Corps standard badge.
2. Naval para qualification badge.
3. Marine cap metal badge.
4. Marine commando qualification badge, awarded by the Sattaship Special Naval Warfare Centre.**

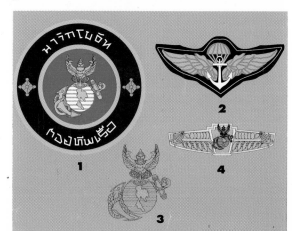

THAI SPECIAL FORCES

Created under US Special Forces' auspices in 1963, the Royal Thai Army's (RTA) Special Forces were based and trained at Lopburi to cope with the internal and external threats faced by this Asian kingdom. In those days, the north of the country, and more particularly the Thai-Malaysian border was infested by powerful communist guerilla movements.

First designated 1st Ranger Battalion, the 580-man strong unit soon changed its name to 1st Special Forces Group and expanded quickly, spawning several sub units (more than 26 SF detachments specialising in anti-guerilla warfare) which eventually grew into regiments. In 1967 Thai volunteers were engaged with American forces (and more particularly the CIA) in Laos during the 'Hardnose' programme. When the Americans pulled out of South Asia in 1975, more than 1,000 Thai SFs had been trained and deployed in Cambodia and in the Vietnamese Highlands as well as being heavily committed in Laos.

The Thais were still fighting the guerillas when in 1976, the SFs joined forces with the US Rangers and border patrol paras in a relentless fight against the communists operating in the southern part of the country.

Modelled on the American units, in 1982 the special forces groups were gathered into the 1st Special Force Divsion and based in the Lopburi region. Its four groups were later expanded into regiments. One year later, the 2nd Special Forces Division was raised in response to the Vietnamese threat in Laos and Kamputchea (formerly Cambodia). In 1985, 3rd Special Forces Regiment was commissioned with 2nd SF Division. Totalling 3,000 men, the SF groups operated within Special Warfare Command, itself answering directly to Thai High Command in Bangkok. The Special Warfare Command had a battalion specialising in psychological warfare, an LRRP deep recce unit, 'Tiger Scouts' intelligence and several elimination teams.

Prior to selection, SF volunteers must be parachute and ranger-qualified. Screening is thorough, resulting in more than 60% of applicants being eliminated during the first three months of tuition. Young and highly motivated, Thai Special Forces are aware that, at the time of trouble, they will be the first to be dispatched into combat. In the final years of the Vietnam War, when Thailand was confronted with hostile communist movements in both Laos and the Khmer Republic, SF teams were used on operations in Khmer Rouge territory and along the northern half of the Khmer border.

With over three decades of combat experience, Royal Thai Special Forces today stand as one of the most capable elite forces in Asia. Trained in action behind enemy lines, sabotage, anti-guerilla and psychological warfare, Thai SF are also tasked with medical and police duties. ❏

A member of Thailand's 1st SF Division, as seen in 1987 on the Kampuchean border. Clad in a locally made black outfit, the man is equipped with US 56 Model webbing with locally-made pouches for 30-round magazines. A combat knife, an M-18 smoke bomb, and two M-59 and M-26 AI fragmentation grenades complete the armament. A ceremonial dagger is suspended from the belt while a machete is strapped to the soldier's back. The Thai is armed with an XM-177E2 assault rifle fitted with a 'Single Point' scope.

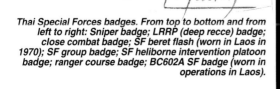

Thai Special Forces badges. From top to bottom and from left to right: Sniper badge; LRRP (deep recce) badge; close combat badge; SF beret flash (worn in Laos in 1970); SF group badge; SF heliborne intervention platoon badge; ranger course badge; BC602A SF badge (worn in operations in Laos).

INDONESIAN PARA

When the Dutch Indies were rocked by unrest in the postwar years, KNILK (*Koninklijk Nederlands Indish Leger Knil* or Dutch Airborne Forces) enlisted many Indonesians to help in their struggle against separatists. From 1946-48, natives were airborne trained by the Dutch Air Force and when Indonesia was given independence in 1950, KNIL and Dutch Air Force-trained personnel formed the cadre of Indonesian airborne units (430th, 454th, and 530th Airborne Battalions, and 100th, 328th, 330th, 531st, 600th and 700th Para-commando Battalions). In 1952, a training school was created in the vicinity of Bandung and three years later, the air force set up its own facilities next to the former at Margahayu.

In 1955, four of these commandos were mustered into the Para-commando Regiment (RPKAD) and deployed within the ground army commando force. In March 1958, one commando unit was dropped over Pakanbaru on Sumatra island to crush rebels and later that month, another unit made an operational jump over Tebing Airport, near Padang. Throughout 1962, RPKAD made several jumps over New Guinea to support the rebels struggling against the Dutch.

To be on an equal par with the army, in 1960 the Indonesian Navy raised a company of parachute-qualified combat divers, quickly followed by the air force, which one year later, set up three Air Force Airborne battalions (PGT). In 1962, PGTs made their operational debut by jumping over New Guinea, again to support rebels fighting the Dutch.

In 1963, the Indonesians found themselves opposed to the British in Borneo and Sarawak, then they turned to Malaysia where the whole Para-commando Regiment was deployed, supported by PGT elements, for operations in the Johore region.

In 1965, RPAKD intervened against mutinous armed forces while the marine regiment further increased its strength by adding three airborne regiments to its complement. One year later, in March 1966, RPAKD participated in the coup that overthrew President Sokarno, irrespective of the fact that for a year, that force and the airborne-trained Presidential Guard (Cakrabirawa) were the President's own bodyguards. One year later, the Para-commando regiment was renamed Kommando Pasukan Sandhi Yudha. In 1972, the airborne units were thoroughly reshuffled and placed under the exclusive command of Koptadra (Air Force Airborne Command). The marines only retained two airborne battalions while the amphibious para-commando recce unit (KIPAM) was turned into a battalion and its units posted to Jakarta, Surabaya and Java.

On 7 December 1976, a RPAKD battalion jumped over East Timor, ready to crush any independence movements that might have sprouted after the Dutch left. Fighting has been going on in this area ever since until the present day.

Indonesia has an impressive airborne force, spearheaded by the 3,000 men of KOPASSUS (Special Forces Group) organised into two commandos and one training company. 17th and 18th Para-commando brigades are backed up by a strategic reserve composed of the four KOSTRAD independent battalions. This force is supported by police (BRIMOB), air force and navy airborne units. Since the creation of the Bandung Airborne School in 1952, Indonesian paras have fought in all counter-insurgency operations, taken part in coups, or joined in the independence struggles against the Dutch and British. ❑

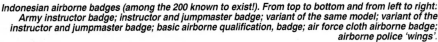

Pictured in Java in 1986, an Indonesian para 'Korporaal' of 2nd Special Forces Para-commando Group (KOPASSUS). Clad in the typical outfit of para-commando units (each has its own camouflage pattern!), the man is issued with locally made webbing, and armed with a West German-manufactured H&K MP5-A2 9mm x 19 submachine-gun. Reknowned for its reliability, this compact weapon is a favourite among elite forces all over the world.

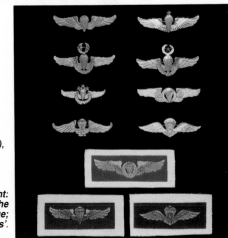

Indonesian airborne badges (among the 200 known to exist!). From top to bottom and from left to right: Army instructor badge; instructor and jumpmaster badge; variant of the same model; variant of the instructor and jumpmaster badge; basic airborne qualification, badge; air force cloth airborne badge; airborne police 'wings'.

SOUTH KOREAN SPECIAL FORCES

South Korean paras originated from the United Nations Partisan Forces Korea, a highly classified Special Operation Force raised in the 1950s during the Korean War for deep recce and sabotage missions behind communist lines (hardly any details about their risky missions have been released). When the conflict ended, the Allies had formed the 1st Airborne Infantry Regiment by combining standard units with the highly specialised teams raised during the conflict.

The missions once carried out by this regiment (and more particularly those assigned to special forces teams) have now been entrusted to Korean special forces.

In the 1970s, the Koreans reaffirmed their staunch commitment to having their own elite units by setting up two airborne brigades (1st and 5th) and three ranger battalions. Quickly known as special forces brigades, these units were modelled on US special forces and still have some US Green Berets as instructors.

Staffed with volunteers and conscripts, Korean SF brigades are organised into one command company and five infantry battalions, each with its own heavy support section. The basic Korean SF sub-unit is the 12-man team.

Western-type training is tough and conducted at the Seongam Special Warfare Centre which functions as both command centre and airborne school. Three SF brigades are designated 'strategic' and are probably meant for cross-border direct action and deep recce. The 1st SF Brigade (based at Kimpo) is known to maintain a HALO deep recce capability and is tasked with airborne assault; the 3rd SF (based at Seongram) may be trained in infiltration in land and sabotage, while the 5th SFD (based at Inchon) is more oriented for underwater action. The other brigades are tactical and probably intended for similiar missions in support of field armies and corps, in addition to organising guerillas in enemy-held territories. The ROK army also conducts a ranger course.

South Korea is obliged to maintain a high number of SF bigades to keep on an equal footing with the North and also fields a sizeable Marine Corps. Formed at Toy Hoa in 1949 under the guidance of US Marines, the ROK Marine Corps had grown into two battalions by the eve of the Korean War. During the war, it expanded into the 1st Marine Corps Regiment (plus some independent units) and later reorganised into brigades. The ROK Marine Corps amounts to 25,000 men, while the Korean Navy has a small combat diver unit specially trained to counter the frequent incursions of their Northern counterparts.

In October 1965, 2nd Marine Corps Brigade 'The Blue Dragoons' arrived in Vietnam and performed with distinction, leaving in February 1972.

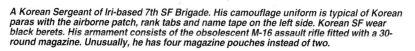

A Korean Sergeant of Iri-based 7th SF Brigade. His camouflage uniform is typical of Korean paras with the airborne patch, rank tabs and name tape on the left side. Korean SF wear black berets. His armament consists of the obsolescent M-16 assault rifle fitted with a 30-round magazine. Unusually, he has four magazine pouches instead of two.

Representative South Korean airborne units badges and insignia. From top to bottom and left to right: Initial airborne badge introduced in the 1950s; air force airborne qualification badge; current senior badge with star, current jumpmaster badge with star and laurel wreath; current basic badge; 1st Brigade badge; Special Forces course badge; current free-faller badge; free-faller team badge.

SOUTH VIETNAMESE PARA

South Vietnamese airborne forces are the oldest on the Asian continent as their history dates back to 1948 when the 1st Indochinese Airborne Company was raised in the former French colony. When Saigon fell to the Communists more than 25 years later, South Vietnamese paras were the last to lay down their arms after fighting the last desperate battle against the communists.

South Vietnam raised an Airborne Group in 1954, shortly after the end of the first Indochina War. Comprising 1st, 3rd, 5th, 6th and 7th Airborne battalions, the new force expanded in 1959 into an airborne brigade after the addition of 2nd and 8th Airborne Battalions, 1st Airborne Artillery Group and three recce companies.

In 1957, American instructors formed the 77th Observation Group - 58 Vietnamese strong - which became Luv Luong Duc Biet (Special Forces) in 1961.

One year previously, 350 men had been selected to compose an Observation Unit, which was converted into 91st Ranger Battalion in 1960. When the war escalated in 1962, paras were constantly in action.

On 1 December 1965, Saigon decided to bolster its airborne forces by creating the 1st Airborne Division (headquartered at Tan-Son-Nut) combining the 1st Brigade (1st, 8th, and 9th Parachute Battalions), the 2nd Brigade (5th, 7th and 11th Parachute Battalions) and the 3rd Brigade (2nd, 3rd and 6th Para Battalions). The three Brigades had one airborne artillery battalion and one recce company each, complemented for 3rd Brigade by one engineer company, and one signal and one surgical unit.

During the war, the paras were deployed as shock troops and fought in most theatres. They made several jumps (one battalion over Bo-Tuc in May 1972, one company over Pleiku in May 1972) but these operations were conducted on a limited scale. Vietnamese paras also operated along the Cambodian border (1970) and in Laos (1971).

In spring 1972, the Division was deployed in the battle of Quang Tri, one of South Vietnam's last ditch attempts to stem the North Vietnamese onslaught. This action cost them 1,000 men killed. When Hué fell in 1975, the 1st Airborne Division fought bitterly to slow down the North Vietnamese Army and was involved in desperate struggles at Xuan-Loc, An Loc and then on through to the ultimate combat in the suburbs of Saigon. After the capitulation, many South Vietnamese paras and ranger units went underground and for many years organised resistance movements against the new regime. ❒

A South Vietnamese para of the 3rd Battalion, 3rd Airborne Brigade at Bien Hoa in 1964. His combat uniform is reminiscent of the 1943 British model widely issued to French airborne troops in Indochina. Badges include the shoulder division patch and the 'winged dagger' on the chest. Maroon beret in hand, the para is equipped with an American helmet and armed with an M1971A2 BAR-Browning light automatic rifle-light machine-gun which, in spite of its size and weight, was widely used by South Vietnamese forces;

South Vietnamese airborne badges. From top to bottom and from left to right: Basic qualification badge; instructor badge; jumpmaster badge with golden palm; airborne qualified ground forces badge; senior badge (awarded after several operational jumps); divisional patch, cap badge; 1st Airborne Division badge.

SOUTH-VIETNAMESE SEAL

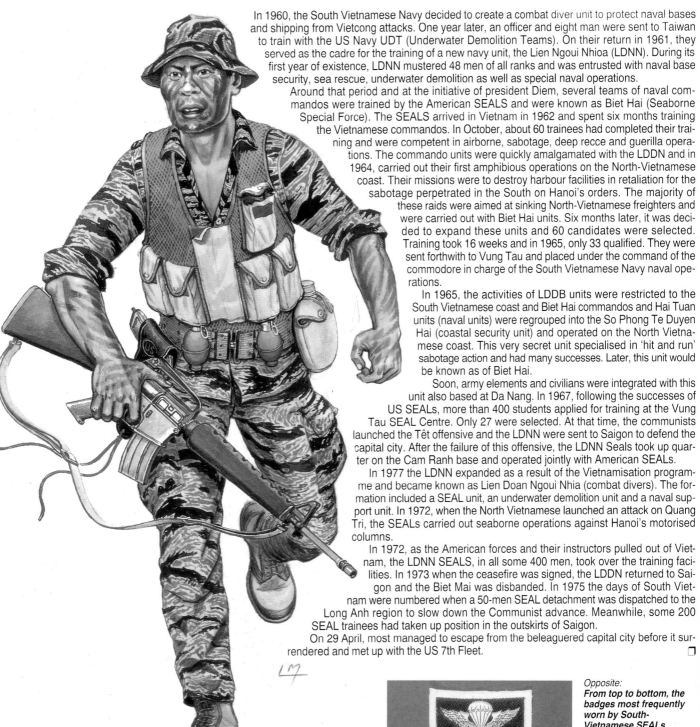

In 1960, the South Vietnamese Navy decided to create a combat diver unit to protect naval bases and shipping from Vietcong attacks. One year later, an officer and eight man were sent to Taiwan to train with the US Navy UDT (Underwater Demolition Teams). On their return in 1961, they served as the cadre for the training of a new navy unit, the Lien Ngoui Nhioa (LDNN). During its first year of existence, LDNN mustered 48 men of all ranks and was entrusted with naval base security, sea rescue, underwater demolition as well as special naval operations.

Around that period and at the initiative of president Diem, several teams of naval commandos were trained by the American SEALS and were known as Biet Hai (Seaborne Special Force). The SEALS arrived in Vietnam in 1962 and spent six months training the Vietnamese commandos. In October, about 60 trainees had completed their training and were competent in airborne, sabotage, deep recce and guerilla operations. The commando units were quickly amalgamated with the LDDN and in 1964, carried out their first amphibious operations on the North-Vietnamese coast. Their missions were to destroy harbour facilities in retaliation for the sabotage perpetrated in the South on Hanoi's orders. The majority of these raids were aimed at sinking North-Vietnamese freighters and were carried out with Biet Hai units. Six months later, it was decided to expand these units and 60 candidates were selected. Training took 16 weeks and in 1965, only 33 qualified. They were sent forthwith to Vung Tau and placed under the command of the commodore in charge of the South Vietnamese Navy naval operations.

In 1965, the activities of LDDB units were restricted to the South Vietnamese coast and Biet Hai commandos and Hai Tuan units (naval units) were regrouped into the So Phong Te Duyen Hai (coastal security unit) and operated on the North Vietnamese coast. This very secret unit specialised in 'hit and run' sabotage action and had many successes. Later, this unit would be known as of Biet Hai.

Soon, army elements and civilians were integrated with this unit also based at Da Nang. In 1967, following the successes of US SEALs, more than 400 students applied for training at the Vung Tau SEAL Centre. Only 27 were selected. At that time, the communists launched the Têt offensive and the LDNN were sent to Saigon to defend the capital city. After the failure of this offensive, the LDNN Seals took up quarter on the Cam Ranh base and operated jointly with American SEALs.

In 1977 the LDNN expanded as a result of the Vietnamisation programme and became known as Lien Doan Ngoui Nhia (combat divers). The formation included a SEAL unit, an underwater demolition unit and a naval support unit. In 1972, when the North Vietnamese launched an attack on Quang Tri, the SEALs carried out seaborne operations against Hanoi's motorised columns.

In 1972, as the American forces and their instructors pulled out of Vietnam, the LDNN SEALS, in all some 400 men, took over the training facilities. In 1973 when the ceasefire was signed, the LDDN returned to Saigon and the Biet Mai was disbanded. In 1975 the days of South Vietnam were numbered when a 50-men SEAL detachment was dispatched to the Long Anh region to slow down the Communist advance. Meanwhile, some 200 SEAL trainees had taken up position in the outskirts of Saigon.

On 29 April, most managed to escape from the beleaguered capital city before it surrendered and met up with the US 7th Fleet.

Above:
A 3rd LDNN South-Vietnamese SEAL in 1972 in the Cam Ranh region. Over his 'tiger stripe' outfit typical of US and South-Vietnamese special forces, the man wears a nylon tactical vest strongly inspired by USAF survival equipment. South-Vietnamese SEALS were always kitted like their American counterparts. The LDNN has supplemented his 30rds magazine M-16A1 with a .45 Colt carried in a holster suspended from his belt. Ranking among Saigon's élite forces, the SEALs inflicted heavy losses on the Vietcong and North-Vietnamese regular forces.

Opposite:
From top to bottom, the badges most frequently worn by South-Vietnamese SEALs. Basic airborne badge (cloth model) LDNN-SEALs chest badge (Red background. Presumably, a green background distinguished special naval units. Colours used for underwater demolition units and sabotage teams would have respectively been blue or orange). US SEAL qualification badge. Most of the South-Vietnamese SEALs were trained by Americans instructors.

JAPANESE PARA

In 1940, 100 German jump instructors arrived to Japan to train a cadre of navy and army airborne personnel. The latter were trained on the island of Hainan while the navy personnel were trained at Kiungshon Base. By December 1941 the students had graduated and, to speed up the process, a further nine traning camps were set up in Japan and China. Soon, about 700 paras had been fully trained and mustered into a special army regiment while the Imperial Navy boasted 1st and 3rd Yokusaka (special naval groups) numbering about 1,000 men.

On 14 February 1942, Japanese paras were dropped over Sumatra to seize the Dutch-held Palembang airfield and seven days later, 3rd Yokusaka jumped over Timor Island and captured Penjoie airfield. The paras' mission was to hold out until the arrival of the marines.

In 1944 1st and 3rd Yokusaka conducted limited actions in China and after merging, the two units were mostly used as elite infantry and fighting the Americans in Saipan. On 6 December 1944, 340 army paras were dropped over Burauen airfield and directly confronted with US Paras of the 101st Airborne Division. The Japanese were beaten and their setback marked the end of Japanese airborne forces.

Japan's 1st Kutei Abn. Brigade was activated in 1955 as the Ground Self Defence Force's parachute unit. Training of the cadre was entrusted to the US 187th Airborne Regimental Combat Team and conducted on Kyushu Island. A parachute school was created in the 1960s, based at Narashino, using American techniques from basic training through to the free-fall course.

Selected after a four-week screening period, Japanese paras are volunteers who attend specialised courses after graduating such as ranger, mountain warfare, combat diving and martial arts.

Japan's airborne force is the 1st 'Kutei' Airborne Brigade, based in the vicinity of Tokyo and fielding 1,200 men organised into one command and three 210-man combat companies as well as several support units. 'Kutei' is the most highly trained unit of the Japanese Self-Defence Forces. ❏

A para of 2nd Company, 1st Airborne Brigade, seen on Hionshu Island before a training jump. He wears the camouflage combat uniform on standard issue to all Japanese forces. The man is equipped with American main and reserve 'chutes as well as the para helmet with typical chin strap. Great care has ben devoted to personal and equipment protection as shown by the extensive padding around the shoulder and the kitbag for the 64 Model 7.62mm assault rifle. The combat bag is worn at knee level. Japanese jump training methods are American inspired.

Japanese airborne qualification badges. From top to bottom and from left to right: Basic qualification badge; fatigues cloth badge; combat uniform cloth badge; combat uniform ranger badge.

CHINESE PARA

In the years between the civil war that preceded World War 2 through to 1949, many US-trained Chinese paras rallied communist forces on the mainland to form the cadre of the future airborne units of the Republic of China. Commissioned in the early 1950s, their prime task was to oppose possible invasion from the Taiwanese Nationalist armies. Some Chinese paras had been battle-hardened in Korea and in the 1960s, the Soviets began to equip two airborne divisions. By 1969, China had three fully-trained airborne divisions which guarded key locations and protected top leaders during the 'cultural revolution'.

In the mid-1980s, Beijing decided to update and reduce considerably the size of its armed forces, but these measures did not affect airborne units, regarded by Chinese Command as the elite 'par excellence'. Currently, the Chinese People's Army fields three airborne divisions (1st, 2nd and 3rd), gathered within the 1st Airborne Corps and integrated within the strategic reserve. The Corps answers to Jinan Military Command near Beijing.

Chinese airborne units normally answer to the air force but can be placed under ground forces' command when necessary. Military experts have established that Chinese airborne units have numerous individual units and special teams trained in deep recce and sabotage actions.

Chinese airborne divisions total 9,000 men, most of them volunteers, and organised into three infantry regiments, one command company, one recce battalion (with free-fallers), one engineer and one artillery battalion, one light air defence battery, as well as one sabotage, one security and one chemical warfare company.

In recent times, the Chinese have made great efforts to update the armament and tactics of their armed forces, and airborne divisions have proven an excellent test bed to try out military techniques imported from the West. China also has three naval infantry divisions including several recce units with combat diver teams.

A paratrooper of the Chinese People's Army belonging to the 1st Division of the 1st Airborne Corps. Issued with the new camouflage utilities introduced in 1986, the man is armed with the ubiquitous folding butt AK-47 and equipped with the famous 'Chi Com' chest webbing. For some years now, the Chinese army has been updating its tactics, and more particularly those of its elite units - sometimes shamelessly adopting western combat techniques.

Chinese airborne qualification badges. Clockwise: current model in air force colours; early Soviet-inspired model; qualification badge awarded to personnel from outside the force.

NEW ZEALAND'S SAS

It was not until June 1955 that New Zealand decided to supplement its armed forces with an airborne unit modelled on the famous British Special Air Service. From the initial 800 applicants who had volunteered for service with the new force, only 138 were selected, and further tests resulted in the elimination of another 49 candidates. On creation, the Squadron totalled 89 men, 40 officers and NCOs. In November, the unit was flown to Malaysia for airborne qualification on Changi Air Base in the vicinity of Singapore, and then received mountain training in the Parak Range, about 250km north of Kuala Lumpur. In 1956, the newly-created NZSAS Squadron was integrated with Britain's 22nd SAS Regiment, and engaged against Malaysian communist guerillas.

After six months of mostly jungle operations, the squadron was reorganised into five platoons which were tasked with tracking and eliminating guerillas, as well as grouping villagers and training them in creating self-defence forces. In the two years spent in Malaysia, the SAS were involved in 14 major engagements and only lost one man killed. In December 1957, the squadron was relieved by an infantry battalion. It was then repatriated and eventually disbanded.

Nine months later, a new SAS unit appeared in New Zealand's order of battle, but the new unit would not not be set up until December 1958.

Composed mostly of 'old hands' from the previous unit, the SAS Platoon was raised to squadron status in 1960, prior to becoming a territorial reserve platoon.

In May 1962, a detachment of 40 SAS was sent to Thailand where it was integrated with US Special Forces under the orders of Major M. Velvin. Based in Korta, the NZSAS trained Thai Rangers and Border Patrol personnel in anti-guerilla warfare.

In commemoration of two native units which distinguished themselves during the Maori Wars, the Forest Rangers and the Taranaki Rangers, the Squadron became officially known in 1963 as New Zealand's 1st SAS Rangers Squadron.

From February 1965 to November 1966, the Squadron's four detachments were rotated to Brunei during the covert war between Borneo and Indonesia. These detachments operated within Britain's 22nd SAS Regiment. In 1965, a training school was created in Auckland as, until then, the NZSAS had to obtain their parachute qualification in Australia.

In November 1968, 4th SAS Platoon was attached to the Australian SAS Regiment and sent to Vietnam. Several platoons were sent to Vietnam on one-year tours and fought the Vietcong. In April 1978, 1st Rangers Squadron became known as 1st SAS Squadron while the training centre became a self-contained unit. Both are now stationed on Papakura Base.

Regardless of rank, all volunteers applying for service with the SAS first undergo a series of pre-selection tests spread over nine days and followed by a week-long selection process. Less than 10% of the candidates of each yearly intake qualify.

The SAS Squadron is trained in recce, commando-type attacks on strategic sites, recovering hostages and prisoners from hosile territories, as well as guerilla and counter-insurgency action.   ❒

Pictured in Papakura, this officer from NZSAS 1st Squadron is kitted out with equipment of British design or inspiration, such as the DPM-type camouflage outfit and the beige beret of British SAS. Only the webbing and the canvas pouch are of American origin. The man is armed with an M-203 assault rifle, providing adequate firepower.

Badges and insignia issued to NZSAS. From top to bottom: Number One Dress shoulder title, beret cloth badge, SAS airborne qualification badge (worn on fatigues), Number One Dress SAS airborne qualification badge. All these badges are practically identical to British models.

AUSTRALIAN SAS

The first Australian SAS unit (1 SAS Company) was created in July 1957 from soldiers who had served with the famous Malayan Scouts (that became 22 SAS in 1952) during the period of unrest that rocked Malaysia from 1948 to 1960. The unit was based at Swanbourne, while a reserve SAS formation was also formed from former paratroopers and named I Battalion, City of Sydney's Own Regiment.

In 1960, the SAS Company was attached to the Royal Australian Regiment but regained its autonomy in 1964 after becoming the fully-fledged Australian SAS Regiment. It took part in numerous exercises in Thailand, New Guinea and Okinawa. In 1965, 1 SAS Squadron was dispatched to Borneo to fight Indonesian troops and was soon joined by 2 SAS Squadron. Around that time, the Australian government decided to send its SAS to Vietnam and from 28 August 1965, 30 Australian SAS started to train villagers in self-defence near Quang Ngai. This training unit soon grew to 100 men. During its Vietnam deployment, the SAS Regiment became I SAS Regiment comprising a support-command unit, a training squadron, 1 and 3 SAS Combat Squadrons, 2 SAS Support Squadron and 151 Signals Squadron. The SAS were mainly involved in anti-guerilla warfare, deep recce missions, and conducted numerous ambushes against the Vietcong. From 1963, 3 SAS Squadron provided mainly deep recce support to the 5th Royal Australian Regiment. In 1970, 3 SAS had accounted for more than 500 Vietcong for the loss of only one man. Indeed, so successful were the Australian SAS that the Americans modelled their own LRRP units (Long Range Reconnaissance and Patrols) on them.

From 1966 to 1971, the Australian SAS operated mainly in the Phuoc Tuy region (south-east of Saigon) where they distinguished themselves and were awarded four Victoria Crosses. 2 SAS Squadron was disbanded after the Vietnam War. Patterned on its British counterpart with which it has close associations, the Regiment also has ties with New Zealand's SBS Squadron. All SAS members are volunteers handpicked from Australian Army units. Selection and training are merciless, eliminating about 80% of applicants. But unlike the British, the Australian armed forces have no marine commandos and so their SAS units devote more time to jungle and amphibious operations as they may be called upon to operate in neighbouring countries where the jungle prevails. In addition to 'classic' missions, Australian SAS are trained in counter-terrorism and are ready to operate in several South-East Asian countries.

Below.
Several Australian SAS qualification badges. Top the Number One suit variant almost identical to the British Malaysian Scouts model and inspired by the SAS airborne badge. Below: one of the badges introduced in the 1970s for wear on the jungle fatigue (a subdued version also exists).

Above.
An Australian SAS soldier of 3 Squadron, pictured in 1988 during an exercise in Queensland. The man is clad in the new jungle fatigues issued to a limited number of units. The efficient camouflage pattern has been designed for Australian bush conditions and for rain forest in which the SAS may have to operate. The other new piece of equipment is the Austrian-manufactured 5.56 x 45 AUG Steyr assault rifle which has been on issue for only two years. This weapon can be used in the submachine-gun, automatic rifle, carbine and light machine-gun roles and is supplied with the appropriate barrels. The assault rifle is fitted with a plastic magazine designed to show the remaining quantity of ammunition. The AUG is fitted with a German-made Luna Tron light amplifying scope. A Plessey PRC-420 transceiver is strapped to the rucksack frame.

AMERICA
(NORTH AND SOUTH)

 CANADA

 UNITED STATES

 GUATEMALA

 EL SALVADOR

VENEZUELA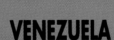

BRAZIL

ARGENTINA

CHILE

Canadian Blue Berets of 22nd Royal
Regiment deployed in Croatia. The
companies of this unit are deployed
in rotation in the airborne role.

CANADIAN PARA

The 1st Canadian Airborne Battalion was raised on 1 July 1942 and one month later, 85 officers, NCOs and men were dispatched to Ringway in Great Britain to attend the airborne course. At the end of 1942, the battalion received further training at Fort Benning, USA. After undergoing a final course at the Shiloh Canadian Airborne School, the paras returned to Great Britain to be integrated with the 3rd Para Brigade, 6th Airborne Division. In June 1944, the battalion jumped over Normandy and was repatriated to Great Britain after the operation. On Christmas Day, it was hurriedly sent to the Ardennes as reinforcement when the Germans launched their last major offensive codenamed 'Wacht am Rhein'. In March 1945, the unit took part in Operation 'Varsity' in support of the Rhine crossings.

Another airborne battalion had also been created in July 1942, but its history followed a totally different course from that of 1st Battalion. Composed of American and Canadian personnel, this unit was designated First Special Service Force and in May 1943, became known as the First Canadian Special Battalion. 1st SSF was blooded in the Aleutian Islands in July 1943, ferried to Sicily in November, then on to Anzio and finally to Provence in 1944 where it spearheaded the landing.

1st SSF was disbanded in January 1945 and all its airborne-qualified members transferred to 1st Battalion.

The Mobile Attack Force (MAF) was raised in 1948 and, interestingly, was composed of three infantry regiments (Princess Patricia's Canadian Light Infantry Regiment, the Royal Canadian Regiment and the Royal 22nd Regiment). For two years, each unit supplied a battalion for airborne operations. Almost exclusively trained for arctic warfare, the Canadians of MAF fought in Korea.

Raised in 1968, the Canadian Airborne Regiment comprised the French-speaking 1st Commando (237 men in 1974), the English-speaking 2nd Commando, and the mixed 3rd Commando formed in 1970. This force was complemented by the 1st Airborne Artillery Battery, the 1st Airborne Engineer Squadron and support elements (headquarters, signals and services). All these units were sent to UN deployments in rotation.

When the Canadian authorities became aware that they needed a rapid intervention force in 1979, they raised the Special Service Force, a light brigade trained for intervention all over the world and capable of operating in all kinds of environment and climatic conditions, from rain forest and desert to the Arctic Circle. SSF included the Canadian Airborne Regiment (three commandos), the 8th Canadian Hussars (an armoured unit) and the First Battalion of the Royal Canadian Regiment.

In addition to these airborne forces answering to the Canadian Army, the Royal Canadian Air Force fields several Para-Rescue units specialising in operations in the far north. ☐

Canadian airborne qualification badges and insignia. From top to bottom and from left to right: airborne metal badge (worn on maroon beret); Para-Rescue cloth qualification badge; airborne qualification badge (worn on fatigues); Special Service Force qualification badge (worn on left shoulder).
Number One dress airborne qualification badge. Top: Princess Patricia Canadian Light Infantry airborne qualification badge, variant of cloth airborne qualification badge (worn on fatigues).

Autumn 1987: a para of First Commando, 1st Canadian Airborne Regiment. British influence can still be seen in the combat outfit (almost identical to the DPM pattern) and the maroon beret. The man shown here is still equipped with the US steel helmet since replaced by the 'Fritz'. This French-speaking para is about to jump and carries a heavy leg bag. Snow shoes for arctic conditions are strapped to the rucksack. On his left shoulder, the Special Service Force patch with the motto 'Osons' (let's dare) can be seen. The CI assault rifle, the locally-built version of the 7.62mm FAL, is strapped to the parachute harness. Canadian paras are also issued with M-16A1/2 assault rifles and with C4M6 Sterling submachine-guns.

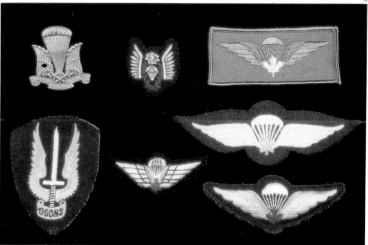

Arctic training for US Marines at Peackle Meadow, near Bridgeport in the Rocky Mountains. When the blizzard blows, temperatures can drop to -35°. In the picture, members of 1st/5th Infantry Regiment are skiing down snowy slopes in a peaceful setting more reminiscent of winter sports than hard training.

US MARINE

'From the Halls of Montezuma to the Shore of Tripoli...' So goes the hymn of the Marines: since 10 November 1775, the Marine Corps - the world's largest elite force - has been involved in all American military ventures across the world. The Marines' first intervention ever took place in Libya in 1805 and was followed by action a few decades later in the 1898 Spanish-American War. Two years later, the Marines were involved in China during the Boxer Rebellion and in 1914, fought at Vera Cruz in Mexico. The Marine Corps distinguished itself again in both World Wars and their actions are remembered in names such as Bois Belleau (1918) and in the 1940s at Guadalcanal, Iwo Jima and Okinawa during the Pacific Campaign. During the Korean War, the 'Leathernecks' stopped the Chinese human waves at Chosin and in 1958, landed for the first time in Lebanon to restore order. Then came Vietnam, where they served for eight years, and fought such celebrated actions at Khe Sanh and Hue, losing 12,936 men killed before pulling out.

In 1965, the Marines landed at San Domingo. In 1975 230 Marines snatched from communists hands the 230 American sailors of USS Mayagez held hostage the Khmer Rouges. In May 1982, the Marines provided a contingent to the international peace-keeping force in Lebanon but the operation was a damp squib - unlike the November 1983 landing at Grenada which turned out to be a complete success.

The US Marine Corps is subdivided into three active and one reserve division with an establishment totalling 184,000 men, 9,200 women and 33,000 reservists. The 1st Marine Division is based at Camp Pendleton on the Pacific Coast, the 2nd at Camp Lejeune on the Atlantic Coast and the 3rd in the Pacific (Hawaii and Okinawa).

The US Marine Corps' combined arms capacity (land, sea and air) and its potential to carry out amphibious operations with the Navy is unique among American forces. The prime task of the USMC is to establish beachheads, secure them and then move inland. Their second mission consists in guarding naval bases and capital battle ships, a task which has been extended to the protection of American officials abroad (embassies etc). In wartime, USMC units are the first to be committed and deployed within the US Rapid Deployment Force, itself subdivided into Marine Amphibious Units (MAU).

Totalling 18,000 men, Marine divisions have 18% more men than their US Army equivalents, and are organised into a triangular pattern of three infantry regiments of three battalions, one artillery regiment, plus one armoured, one amphibious and one assault battalion (equipped with light armoured vehicles). The three divisions have their own recon forces, special units to explore landing sites covertly before amphibious operations.

All volunteers and professionals, future-Marines are directed to the San Diego (California) and Parris Island (South Carolina) camps for the infamous training period which will turn them into 'Leathernecks'. The 'boots' (recruits) are left to the care of the dreaded DIs (drill instructors) who, for 11 weeks, will instil into them the obediance, discipline and basic military skills which have always been the hallmark of the Marine Corps.

Although a sizeable force, the Corps doesn't have its own academy and all officers must graduate from the Annapolis Naval Academy before tackling the rigorous course at Quantico prior to being commissioned with the USMC. ❑

1983: armed with an M-203 grenade launcher, a grenadier on duty in Lebanon. Over his BDUs, he wears the new PASGT (Personal Armor System, Ground Troops) vest, made of Kevlar with bullet resistance properties. The pack and LC-1 equipment together comprise the ALICE set now in use by all US forces.

USMC insignia and badges. Top, from left to right: USMC strip, with the 1st and 2nd Marine Divisions patches. Centre: the famous USMC headgear metal badge displayed above the 1983 Lebanon commemorative patch flanked by the 3rd and 5th Marine Division patches.

With an M-16A2 assault rifle in hand, a Marine Recon during a patrol through the lush vegetation in Camp Lejeune, Florida.

MARINE RECON

In July 1941, some 225 US Marines won their 'parachute'wings' after training at the Lakehurst naval/air base. One month later, on 15 August, the Marine Corps created the First Parachute Battalion, followed in October by the Second Battalion. Shortly thereafter, 1st Battalion was sent to the Pacific and in summer 1942, was involved in the Guadalcanal campaign against the Japanese. US command was so impressed by the airborne unit's performance that it created the Third Parachute Battalion in September 1942.

On 1st April 1943, the three battalions were amalgamated into the First Parachute Regiment, and were used as elite infantry in Bougainville, before taking an active part in the recapture of numerous Pacific Islands until January 1944. In February 1944, the regiment was disbanded but retained as cadre for the 5th Marine Brigade.

Deep-recce units designated 'raiders' had also been raised, and in August 1942, 1st Raider Battalion fought in Guadalcanal alongside 1st Para Marine Battalion. In March 1942, the four raider battalions were grouped into the 1st Marine Raider Regiment. These special units were heavily involved in the recapture of many islands, only to be disbanded in January 1944 after the operation in the Solomon Islands.

Although the Marine Corps had disbanded its special units in 1944, Marines were still undergoing airborne training at Camp Lejeune prior to being attached to the two amphibious recce companies of the First (Atlantic) and Second (Pacific) Fleets.

In 1957, 1st Amphibious Reconnaissance Company became 1st Force Reconnaissance Company and was sent to Vietnam where it operated from October 1965 to August 1970. A further two units were then set up. From April 1967 to August 1970, 3rd Company fought in Vietnam within the 3rd Marine Division. These units were then redesignated 'Marine Recon'. Currently, the Marine Corps fields three Marine Recon Battalions attached to the 1st, 2nd

and 3rd Marine Divisions, but answering directly to the Atlantic and Pacific Fleet Marine Forces. Each battalion comprises four companies (plus one reserve company that can be deployed in wartime), and each company comprises three platoons. Four teams of four men constitute a platoon. Regarded as the elite of the USMC, Recon Marines are selected after serving two years with the Corps. Applicants are handpicked, and on top of being parachute-qualified, each man has several specialities.

Like most special forces, Recon Marines keep out of the limelight. ▢

*Above: **A Recon Marine from 5th Marine Expeditionary Brigade seen in January 1991 during the deployment in Kuwait. Wearing a black BDU, the man has just returned from a recce mission though Iraqi lines. Over his outfit, the man wears a Cordura assault vest with seven ammo pouches. He is armed with a sound-suppressed 9mm HK-MP 5 SD-3 submachine gun. This highly efficient weapon is issued to numerous special units all over the world. On this forehead, the man has AN/PVS-5A light intensifying scopes.***

*Opposite. **Several Marine Recon badges and speciality insignias From top to bottom and from left to right: Vietnam Marine Recon Parachute Qualification badge, variant of the same badge, World War Two 1st Marine Amphibious Corps Raiders badge, Current Marine Recon parachute qualification badge, battledress airborne qualification badge, current 1st Recon Battalion Badge.***

Marine Recons of 4th MEB explore the landing site of the Jaek' Kevarri peninsula during a training exercise in Norway. The LCACs (landing craft air cushion) brought the assault troops ashore less than one hour after the Marines had been delivered by CH-46 and CH-53 helicopters.

SEALs completing a training exercise. The assault on Patilla Airport had been rehearsed many times at home and in Panama but this time, the objective was real. The success of Operation 'Just Cause' and the downfall of General Noriega depended on the capture of the airport.

US SEAL

Although the SEAL teams were officially commissioned on 1 January 1962 by President Kennedy, the creation of this famous amphibious force dates back to 1942 when a 17-man detachment known as NCDU (Navy Combat Demolition Unit) was raised by the US Navy to deal with maritime and beach obstacles.

Their first mission took place on 11 November 1942 when 16 UDT (Underwater Demolition Team) divers blasted the way open for Allied landings in North Africa. Other teams were active at the same time in the Pacific theatre and, in June 1944, UDTs cleared the beaches and harbours during the amphibious operations in Normandy.

Most UDTs were decommissioned after World War 2, but the few that remained active saw action during the Korean War and took part in sabotage and recce missions against harbours in Communist China. In 1955, UDTs were based in the T'aichung Islands in Nationalist China and later transferred to Subic Bay in the Philippines. It was then that UDT Command decided to broaden the scope of their duties and have them operate along similar lines as the USMC's Marine recons who fight ashore after beaching.

The Vietnam War gave the SEALs the opportunity they needed to make the most of their skills and, during the five-year campaign, they successfully completed 153 major missions and accounted for more than 1,000 Vietcong killed and 1,000 captured for the loss of only one man. After Vietnam, they returned to the USA and took part in numerous NATO exercises. Gradually, all UDTs were converted and combined into SEAL teams and, in 1983, the SEALs took part in Operation 'Just Cause' in Grenada. In 1989, they captured Panama City's strategic airport and in February 1991, were the first allied soldiers to enter Kuwait City.

Answering to USSCOM, SEAL units are organised into Naval Special Warfare Group 1 (Pacific, based at Coronado, California) and Naval Special Warfare 2 (Atlantic, based at Little Creek, Virginia). Each NSWG consists of three SEAL teams, three Special Boat Units, one SEAL Delivery Vehicle Team and one Light Attack Helicopter Squadron. Specialising in anti-terrorist action, SEAL Team 6 is permanently attached to Delta Force and comes under Joint Special Operations Command Control. In addition, there are Naval Special Warfare Units in Scotland, the Philippines and Portugal. The force totals 2,900 men and a full SEAL team numbers 27 officers and 156 petty officers and seamen distributed into five platoons. SEAL training is astonishingly hard with barely half the candidates staying the distance (more than 80% have already been eliminated through preliminary screening). The course calls for mental toughness and iron willpower; during the infamous 'Hell Week' (Week 6 of the course) trainees only get four hours sleep in six days!

Spread over several years, the SEAL course involves all aspects of amphibious recce and raiding as well as HALO and HAHO parachute techniques. The SEALs constitute the elite of US amphibious forces and are highly regarded by other similar units. ❏

Vietnam 1967. During the most active period of the US Navy Special Forces' history, a member of SEAL Team in action in the Delta. Answering to MACV/SOG (Military Assistance Command Vietnam/Study and Observation Group), the man is shown here in the famous 'tiger stripes' uniform topped off by a camouflage bandanna. The webbing M-16 pouches were more commonly used for carrying water canteens and various paraphenalia. Elite forces have always enjoyed more freedom in choosing their equipment as demonstrated by the SEAL's weapons: slung over his shoulder is a 5.56mm Stoner M-63 light machine-gun on widespread issue among SEALs and fitted with a 160rds box magazine. The handgun he is firing a sound-suppressed 9mm Mk 22 Smith and Wesson fitted with a 'Hush Puppy' silencer. This weapon came in handy whenever Vietcong sentries had to be stealthily eliminated. A Randall combat knife, specifically designed for US Special Forces, is fastened upside down to the front of the left webbing brace.

Various SEAL patches. From left to right: SEAL Team 1 patch, SEAL Team 2 patch, SEAL Team 3 patch, qualification badge; SEAL Team 4 and SEAL Team 5 (not shown here are the badges of SEAL Teams 6, 7 and 8)

US NAVY SBS

The US Navy had contemplated the creation of specialised teams trained in delivering and recovering Underwater Demolition Teams during World War 2 but the project never got past the planning stage. In the Pacific theatre, UDTs were delivered by torpedo boats or from submarines surfacing off Japanese-held islands.

A few decades later, the Vietnam War and the efficiency of SEAL teams gave the USN the opportunity to re-initiate the programme and set up units capable of delivering SF teams to the operational zone - and recovering them without fuss.

A small flotilla was created in 1966 and initially issued with small, civilian craft. Ideal for river and Delta marshy conditions, these small boats were driven by SEALs who praised their substantial range and stealth. They were primarily involved in deep recce, anti-guerilla warfare and laying booby traps on tracks and around enemy camps.

Impressed by their success, the force was boosted (more than 200 SEALs were deployed!) by creating four special boat units that were later gathered into Special Boat Squadron 1.

Several types of boats were issued: the IBS (Inflatable Boat Small); the longer, heavier and faster LCPL (Landing Craft Personnel Launch) fitted with a 300hp engine and later, the 5m long Boston Whaler propelled by a 40-80hp motor. Also ideal for commando delivery were the Stab (8m, two 325hp engines) and the larger and better armed MSSC (Medium SEAL Support Craft which was 11m long with two 325hp engines). More recently, the new, faster 11m Seafox has been added to the range along with the amazing Excalibur that can operate on the surface and at depths of up to 60m. (The latter was used during the Gulf War to deliver underwater recce teams to the Kuwaiti shore.)

Currently, two SBSs (Special Boat Squadron) and six SBUs (Special Boat Unit) are on strength with the US Navy's two Special Warfare Groups (NAVSPECWARGRU 1 and 2).

Based at Coronado, San Diego, SBS 1 comprises SBU 11, based on Marc Island, California (also home to a reserve SBU), and Coronado-based SBU 12 and 13. A detachment of SBS1 is deployed at Subic Bay in the Philippines. Stationed at Little Creek, a small naval base at Norfolk, Virginia, SBS 2 comprises SBU 21 and 23, while SBU 22 is based in New Orleans and serves a reserve and cadre unit. SBS 2's advanced base is at Puerto Rico.

All applicants for SEAL, UDT and SBS service are put through the same stringent selection procedure and training which is spread over 23 weeks (the first four are devoted to psychological and physical selection while the fifth one, unofficially known as 'motivation week' will determine the admission of the candidate).

Serious business then starts on San Clemente island with the trainees being coached in raids, guerilla warfare, demolition and underwater swimming. Usually, airborne and combat diver qualifications are obtained one after the other (most SEALs are free-fall qualified). With training behind them, the fully-fledged SEALs are now commissioned with an active unit where further skills, such as SBU techniques, will be acquired. Navigation, communication and maintenance courses are also a prerequisite for SEALs who must be able to carry out a sabotage mission and drive a subskimmer with closed circuit aqualung on.

The prime mission of SBUs is to insert SEAL teams as close as possible to their objectives - be it on a beach or up a river - then to recover them while providing whatever fire support is required. ❑

A member of SBU 21 during the 1990 Operation 'Desert Shield'. For several months SEALs and Royal Navy SBS explored the Kuwaiti coastline and the Euphrates Delta. To drive his Excalibur 180 subskimmer, the diver is equipped with a closed circuit Emerson back aqualung and wears an NV-700 underwater vision system derived from the US Army AN/PVS-7A night vision equipment. He is armed with a Swedish-made 9mm M-45 Carl Gustav submachine-gun, a favourite among American Special Forces.

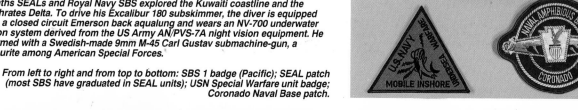

From left to right and from top to bottom: SBS 1 badge (Pacific); SEAL patch (most SBS have graduated in SEAL units); USN Special Warfare unit badge; Coronado Naval Base patch.

USAF SPECIAL FORCES (CCT)

The US Air Force has several Special Forces units, organised into squadrons, operating within 23rd Air Force and controlled by 1st Special Operation Wing (1st SOW). In the same way as all US Army and Navy special units, 1st SOW answers to Joint Special Operations Command and is subdivided into three squadrons, each with its own CCT (Combat Control Team) trained for close observation, objective identification and drop zone marking. A relatively new and little publicized force, these units operate broadly along the same lines as the World War 2 'Pathfinders'. A team of Pathfinders was attached to each American airborne regiment and was dropped before the main assault to mark out the drop zone and direct the aircraft. Pathfinders operated successfully during the Korean War and later again in Vietnam. During the latter conflict, when American involvement peaked in the late 1960s, each aviation group had its own combat control teams. CCTs had other duties: deep recce in Vietcong-held territory involving night jumps, selecting landing sites for airmobile forces and guiding attack aircraft to targets.

Taking its cues from the army, the US Air Force created CCT units in 1956 and during the Vietnam War, deployed them alongside special forces taking part in the CIDG (Civilian Irregular Defense Group) programme. Scattered all over enemy-held territory, the CCTs' prime duties were the co-ordination of air supply and combat control. In the 1970s, the scope of USAF CCTs' missions was broadened thanks to the introduction of improved electronic systems allowing for more accuracy. The CCTs were intensively committed in the US interventions in Grenada and Panama. Their latest wartime mission took place during 'Desert Storm' when about a dozen teams operated behind Iraqi lines deep inside enemy territory. The CCTs had the considerable task of identifying objectives and, along with other US Special Forces, marking out landing zones for the 101st Air Assault helicopters as well as setting up beacons for bombers.

The USAF fields about 300 combat controllers, wearing the prestigious maroon beret. The volunteers are selected from among USAF Air Control School or USAF active units. CCT candidates undergo an 18-week screening period at the Keesler Air Control School, which eliminates about 50% applicants, before attending a more specialised eight-week course at Pope, North Carolina. After obtaining the airborne qualification (fivre jumps) at Fort Bragg, the future combat controllers are trained in communications, armament, ambushes, landing zone marking and heli-transport action. In addition, all Controllers hold the airborne instructor rating, are physically fully trained and must be thoroughly knowledgeable about US Federal Aviation procedures.

Home-based CCT units are quartered at Hurburt, Little Rock and Norton, while those on overseas duties are deployed at Clark (Philippines); Howard (Panama) and Rhein Main (Germany). ❑

February 1991, a combat controller in action somewhere in Iraqi territory during Operation 'Desert Shield'. Delivered at night by a 1st Special Operations Wing helicopter, the controller is about to set up beacons for American bombers. His equipment is standard US issue except for the impressive rucksack containing enough rations to see him through 10 days of combat.

128

USAF airborne qualification badges (1956-63). From left to right and from top to bottom: Combat Control Team cap badge; Air Weather Service badge (issued to weather specialists opeating behind enemy lines); 1st Special Operation Wing shoulder tab; 7th Special Operation Squadron shoulder tab (based at Bad Tölz in Germany); 605th Air Commando Squadron flash; Air Weather Service cap flash (worn with the metal badge placed above).

ARRS PARA-RESCUEMAN

Created on 13 March 1946, the Aerospace Rescue and Recovery Service (ARRS) currently answers to the US Air Force's Air Transport Command. Belonging to one of the world's lesser known special forces units, the Para-Rescuemen (PJ or Para Jumpers) rank none-the-less among the most highly trained personnel, capable of tackling most situations. Their prime mission consists in searching for and rescuing airmen who have gone down over land or sea (often behind enemy lines or under fire). Their first operation of this type took place in August 1943 in Burma and was followed by many more throughout the Pacific War.

In 1948, ARRS was placed under the control of MATS (Military Airlift Transport Service) later known as Military Airlift Command (MAC). During the Korean War, the ARRS paras rescued more than 996 pilots and aircrew. But the heyday of this special unit began in April 1962 with the arrival of six Para-Rescuemen in Vietnam. Originally, rescue missions were made from helicopters provided by the US Marines and the US Army but in 1965, the unit received its HH-3E 'Jolly Green Giant' helicopters, which were followed by 'Super Giants' and deployed on the air bases of Bien Hoa, Da Nang, Udorn, Nakhon Phanom, Takhli and Korat.

The PJs soon developed their own rescue technique, known as SARTAF, involving two helicopters hovering over the downed aircraft while propeller-driven aircraft (usually four) neutralised ground opposition (because of their higher speed, jets were not as well suited for these types of assignment). In operation, the lowest 'chopper' rescued the downed airmen while the other was kept on stand-by, ready to intervene in case things went wrong. In June 1966, the 3rd Aerospace Rescue and Recovery Group took up quarters at Tan Son Nhut and was placed under the command of the Joint Search and Rescue Centre that supervised all air rescue operations over Laos, Cambodia and Vietnam. 3rd ARRG was subdivided into four squadrons, 37th at Da Nang, 38th at Tan Son Nhut, 39th at Tuy Hoa and 40th at Udorn.

The PJs had their busiest time in 1968 when the US Air Force embarked on a major bombing offensive against communist forces in South and North Vietnam. That year, a total of 916 pilots and aircrew were rescued. When the ARRS paras left Vietnam in 1973, they had saved more than 3,883 men for the loss of 73 of their number and 45 aircraft.

On 1 March 1983, all the USAF special units were grouped within MAC and currently, ARRS is equipped with 160 transport aircraft and 50 helicopters. The unit numbers 3,800 servicemen and women. In addition to its air rescue missions, ARRS assists NASA with the recovery of astronauts. Parachute-qualified and wearing the maroon beret of airborne forces, all the PJs are volunteers who have attended the combat diver course and been through the survival schools run by the USAF in Panama. All Para-Rescuemen have received medical training and obtained the Ranger qualification. ❑

A USAF Para Jumper sergeant undergoing the jungle survival course in 1987 in Panama. The man wears the old 'duck hunter' pattern overall and holds a crash helmet, an indispensable protection when winching in and out of helicopters. Unusually, the man has donned his red beret (preferably worn with Number One dress) and displays the latest M-9 combat knife privately purchased from the PX. He is armed with an M-16A2 Model 733 Commando assault rifle, and carries the ubiquitous Colt 45 (soon to be phased out).

USAF Para-Rescue badges and insignia. Centre and from top to bottom: ARRS cap metal badge; standard airborne badge, USAF aircrew badge. On either side, the ARRS cloth badges (Number One dress and fatigue variants).

US RANGER

In May 1942, American General Truscott petitioned US High Command about the creation of an American special unit which would operate along the same lines as the British Commandos. This special force was named 'Rangers' in commemoration of the famous American units of War of Independence fame.

In June 1942, the 1st Ranger Battalion was created in Great Britain from volunteers and trained in Scotland (about 50 of these men took part in the ill-fated Dieppe landing in August of that year.)

While the 2nd US Ranger Battalion was formed in the United States, 1st Battalion landed in North Africa in November 1942 after undergoing the same training as British Commandos. The Rangers were involved in fierce fighting against the Afrika Korps around the famous Kasserine Pass. After its losses had been made good, 1st Battalion bolstered by 3rd and 4th Battalions, landed in Sicily (March 1943) to clear the high ground overlooking the beachhead. In January 1944, the Rangers lived through hell at Anzio where 1st and 3rd Battalions suffered 60% losses.

Meanwhile, 2nd Battalion had been ferried to Great Britain and later played a significant part in the Normandy landings by capturing the formidable clifftop positions of Pointe du Hoc. After the breakthrough, 5th and 2nd Battalions fought on all the way to Germany's heartland prior to being disbanded in May 1945. Trained for the Pacific theatre, 6th Battalion fought in New Guinea (August 1944) and landed in the Philippines. That unit was disbanded in Japan in December 1945.

When reactivated for the Korean War (1950-53), the Rangers fielded more than 15 companies, attached to various divisions and specialising in deep recce and forays behind enemy lines. The Ranger units were disbanded shortly after the war ended but this didn't stop their training school from issuing the specific qualifications of this elite force. In 1975, 1st and 2nd Battalions of the 75th Infantry Regiment (1/75 and 2/75) were reactivated, preceding the creation of the 3rd Battalion (3/75) in 1984.

On 25 October 1983, several hundreds of Rangers from 1/75 and 2/75 were dropped at dawn over Grenada and seized Cuban-held Port Malines airport, paving the way for the paras of 82nd Airborne Division to make a successful landing. Currently, 75th Ranger is divided into three battalions, each numbering 610 men and organised like any other similar US Army unit into three infantry and one command company.

1/75 is based at Hunter (Georgia), 2/75 at Fort Lewis (Washington) and 3/75 the at Fort Benning (Georgia) also home to the Ranger training school. As in all special Forces, Ranger selection is very stringent although conducted on a different basis: after successfully passing the primary selection tests, candidates are commissioned with an active unit and serve for a year before taking up training proper. Success rate is about 50%. During selection, emphasis is placed on character, performance and progression during the first eight weeks of the course. Rangers, who average 20-22 years of age, are then returned to their unit and allowed to wear the prestigious black beret.

In spite of the particular nature of their missions, Rangers are issued with standard armament, ranging from M-1, M16A1/2 and CAR-15 (for radio operators and officers) to the SAW (Squad Automatic Weapon) and M-203 grenade launchers. Each company is issued with a 60mm mortar. The Rangers' heaviest weapon is the recoilless 90mm gun. ❏

October 1983: a US Ranger of 1/75 in Grenada. The man is clad in tropical fatigues, wears jungle boots and is issued with all purpose lightweight individual combat equipment. The man's headgear is an OD51 cap sporting the Airborne and Ranger patches. The 2/75 Ranger Battalion insignia is worn on the shoulder. His weapon, an M-203 grenade launcher endows him with considerable firepower. The Ranger carries 40mm explosive and fragmentation ammunition in the pouches of a specifically designed load carrying vest.

Some representative US Rangers badges displayed around the 75th Infantry Regiment oval insignia and airborne qualification badge: subdued variant of the shoulder patch (left) and the model worn on the number one dress (right). Second row: 1970-80 1st Battalion shoulder patch; the 75th beret flash with metal badge (introduced on 20 August 1970); the 1970-80 2nd Battalion shoulder patch, and the 1984 3rd Battalion shoulder patch.

*A recce team of F Coy, 51st Infantry
Regiment during a training exercise. The
unit is based at Ludwigsburg, Germany,*

US 82ND PARA

Grenada, October 1983. Since 1979, American paras have been issued with maroon berets adorned with their unit patch as shown by this sniper, a corporal of 1/508th Infantry, 82nd Airborne. His camouflage BDU has the woodland pattern and his M-21 7.62mm sniper rifle is fitted with a Redfield scope.

The activation of the US Army's first parachute unit - the Parachute Test Platoon - was authorised on 25 June 1940 and the unit formed at Fort Benning from 29th Infantry Regiment personnel. The platoon numbered two officers and 48 men, selected from the 200 who had volunteered. The first mass jump was made on the 29th. These paras formed the cadre of airborne units and from 1941, trained the 501st, 502nd, 503rd and 504th Parachute Infantry Battalions. In 1942, these units grew into three-battalion regiments. 1942 was a decisive year in the history of the American airborne forces when all units were placed under a common command and two divisons (82nd All American and 101st Screaming Eagles) were created. In November 1942, the 509th Battalion made the first operational jump of the war over North Africa. The forces expanded in 1943 with the creation of another three divisions (11th 'Angels', 13th 'Black Cats', and 17th 'The Talon').

After making operational jumps over Sicily and Italy, the 82nd was reunited in Britain with the 101st in time for the Normandy landings. In June 1944, the 101st Division and the 82nd Division were bolstered by the 12th Airborne Brigade for the operation. Meanwhile, the 11th was dispatched to the Pacific while the 17th completed training and the 13th was undergoing a thorough reshuffle.

On 6 June 1944, the 82nd and 101st Brigades jumped over the Normandy *'bocage'* and, in spite of very high losses, successfully accomplished their mission. In August 1944, US and British paras combined into the 1st Airborne Task Force were dropped over Provence. In September, 82nd and 101st took part in the ill-fated Operation 'Market Garden' at Arnhem. US paras fought through until the end of the war mostly deployed as elite infantry. They are remembered for their gallant action at Bastogne (101st) and Elba (82nd) in particular.

Two American airborne units, the 11th Airborne Division and 503 Airborne Regiment, were meanwhile deployed in the Pacific. The latter made three operational jumps, the most famous over Corregidor in February 1945.

When the Korean War broke out in 1950, the 187th Airborne Regiment made two jumps to stem the Chinese human waves. In April 1965, the 82nd Division landed at San Domingo to restore order. Three years later, the 82nd Division's 3rd Brigade was sent to Vietnam for a 22-month tour and took part in numerous actions until relieved by the 4th Brigade in December 1969. In 1983, the 2nd Brigade was dropped over Grenada and, in a few days, had overcome Cuban resistance.

Deactivated and reactivated several times, the 101st Airborne was sent to Vietnam in summer 1965 and distinguished itself in many actions (for example the January 1968 Tet Offensive). In July 1969, the unit was converted into the 101st Airmobile Division and deployed in Vietnam until 1972. Meanwhile, the 173rd Airborne Brigade took part in all the major search and destroy operations and recorded the first operational jump made by American forces since the Korean War.

Currently, the 82nd is America's sole remaining airborne division and spearheads the US Rapid Deployment Force, whereas the 101st specialises in heliborne assault. Based at Fort Bragg in North Carolina, the two divisions operate within the XVIIIth Airborne Corps.

Top row from left to right: three US airborne qualification badges (basic, senior and jumpmaster). Top row: subdued variants, second row: walk-out dress models. The basic badge is awarded after five jumps while the 'senior' is awarded after 30 (including 15 with full kit and two by night as well as achieving the instructor rating). A total of 56 jumps is required to obtain the 'jumpmaster' (25 with full kit, two by night and five tactical jumps) in addition to the instructor rating and 36-months active service in a para unit. Bronze stars indicate operational jumps.

US 101ST PARA

Raised in 1942 and commanded by General Lee, the 101st Airborne Division ('Screaming Eagles') came into being a few days after its sister unit, the 82nd Division ('All American'). Reinforced by the 501st, and 506th PIR (Parachute Infantry Regiment), the Division was sent to Britain for the Normandy landings. During the night of 5-6 June 1944, they jumped over the *'bocage'* with their leader, General Maxwell Taylor. The rest of the unit was dropped as reinforcements after the landing, losses were heavy and by mid-July, when the 101st returned to Britain, its strength was down to 50%. In September 1944, the 'Screaming Eagles' took part in Operation 'Market Garden' at Arnhem where their mission was to capture and hold the Eindhoven and Veghel bridges. There again, losses were high.

In December, the Division was hurriedly dispatched to the Belgian town of Bastogne in the Ardennes. Encircled and subjected to severe bombings, the paras held out against all odds until relieved by US forces, thus recording one of the most glorious achievements in the Division's history. The Division was repatriated to the United States after Germany's surrender and became a reserve unit in late 1945.

Between 1948 and 1956, the Division was reactivated three times as a cadre unit and on 21 September 1956, was commissioned as an active division with five combat regiments, five artillery batteries and five command and support battalions.

On 25 July 1956, the 1st Brigade (reorganised into three combat brigades with support units) was deployed in Vietnam and integrated with Task Force 'Oregon' (comprising: 101st Division's 1st Brigade, 25th ID 3rd Brigade and 196th Infantry Brigade). By November 1967, the 101st Division was collected together where its missions rapidly evolved from the airborne to the airmobile role (US command felt that massive use of helicopters could increase the mobility of airborne units).

In August 1968, the the 101st Division officially became 101st ABN Division (airmobile) and its brigades were heavily committed in all major operations against the Vietcong. On 10 March 1972, the last 'Screaming Eagles' left Vietnam for Fort Campbell.

Currently, the 101st Brigade belongs to the Rapid Deployment Force and operates within the XVIII Airborne Corps. Redesignated Air Assault in 1977, the 101st Division is the US Army's sole heliborne assault unit. Organised into eight combat regiments, one free-faller company, three artillery, one air defence and one engineer battalion, the Division also has an air brigade, a transport (Blackhawk), an attack (Apache and Cobra) and liaison and recce units (Apache and Kiowa).

A truly unique force, the 101st ABN Division served as the model for British, French and Soviet airmobile units.   ❒

A para of the 101st Airborne Division (Air Assault), in Saudi Arabia during Operation 'Desert Shield'. Clad in the spotted camouflage combat uniform widely issued to GIs during this operation, the 'Screaming Eagle' wears a matching flak jacket and is armed with a 5.56mm SAW M-249 light machine-gun. With the exception of the goggles strapped to the 'Fritz' helmet, his equipment is standard 'Central Europe' issue. The NBC bag fastened to the leg and the smoke grenades dangling from the webbing are especially noteworthy.

101st Airborne Division badges. From left to right and from top to bottom: 503rd Airborne Infantry Regiment patch; 101st Airborne Division patch; 'Air Assault' oval qualification badge with the colours of 101st Airborne Division HQ; 502nd Airborne Infantry Regiment patch; 187th Airborne Infantry Regiment patch.

137

Members of the 82nd Airborne Division pictured somewhere to the north of Dharan during Operation 'Desert Storm'. This unit was the first to arrive in the Gulf .

American paras of the 325th Airborne Regiment during an Allied Mobile Force exercise. This regiment is based in Italy.

US SPECIAL FORCES

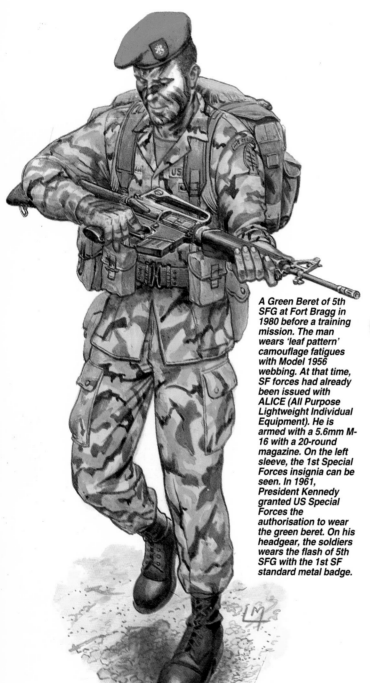

A Green Beret of 5th SFG at Fort Bragg in 1980 before a training mission. The man wears 'leaf pattern' camouflage fatigues with Model 1956 webbing. At that time, SF forces had already been issued with ALICE (All Purpose Lightweight Individual Equipment). He is armed with a 5.6mm M-16 with a 20-round magazine. On the left sleeve, the 1st Special Forces insignia can be seen. In 1961, President Kennedy granted US Special Forces the authorisation to wear the green beret. On his headgear, the soldiers wears the flash of 5th SFG with the 1st SF standard metal badge.

In July 1943 Allied High Command decided to emulate the British by creating a Special Forces unit with Canadian and American personnel. After a drastic selection process, the soldiers were commissioned with the 1st Special Service Force, a unit specialising in raids behind enemy lines. Placed under the orders of Col Frederick, 1st Special Service Force comprised three regiments of two battalions each.

After an amphibious operation against the Japanese-held Aleutian Islands in Alaska, the three regiments were dispatched to Italy in December 1943. In February 1944, they landed in the Anzio inferno and fought their way to Rome. On 14 August 1944, 1st SSF took part in the Allied landings in Provence before the force was disbanded in December.

The Special Forces were reactivated when 10 Special Forces Group was set up at Fort Bragg in 1952. The following year, 77th Special Forces Group was created with elements from the 10th. The cold war was then in full swing and the Special Forces' main mission was to operate in enemy territories where they would be sent to create and organise underground resistance forces. South America, Asia and Eastern Europe were seen as their most likely areas of operation. At this time more volunteers from Central Europe were recruited to perform these tasks behind the Iron Curtain.

In June 1957, 58 men from Okinawa-based 1st SFG (mostly 77st SFG cadre members), were dispatched to South Vietnam to train Saigon's Rangers. This marked the beginning of the long involvement of US Special Forces in Vietnam which actually lasted until 1975 (although official records would prefer us to believe 1971). US Special Forces were sent to Vietnam in September 1961 when 5th SFG was deployed there and entrusted with all special operations. To counter the Vietcong, several defence programmes were initiated, including the training of villagers (CIDG or Civilian Irregular Defence Groups) and the Delta programme involving deep recce and sabotage, and aimed at eradicating the infrastructure of the Vietcong.

Better known as 'Green Berets', the SF conducted deep forays into the heartland of Vietnam (Son Tay raid etc). In 1965, Special Forces' numbers reached an all-time peak with the creation of 8th SFG, 6th SFG and 2nd SFG respectively trained for action in South America, the Middle East and Africa. In 1961, 1st, 7th and 10th SFG were gathered into 1st Special Forces and their missions no longer restricted to Vietnam. From 1963 to 1970, more than 500 SF teams were dispatched to 19 countries to train local Special Forces.

The 1971-83 era was a period of lean times for US Special Forces until the growing threat of international terrorism prompted the Pentagon to boost their ranks again and reshuffle the units. After revamping, each group mustered three operational battalions bringing the total of US Special Forces to 5th and 7th SFG (Fort Bragg), 10th SFG (Fort Devens), 1st SFG (Fort Lewis), 1/10 SFG (Bad Tolz), 4th Psychological Operation Group and 96th Civil Affairs (Fort Bragg). In 1982, all these units were placed under the control of 1st Special Operations Command (SOCOM).

Green Berets must be the best in their field and are handpicked after a 17-week selection that eliminates more than one third of applicants. This is followed by specialised courses. The basic SF unit is a 12-man team, with four teams making up a detachment, and four detachments a company. The SF group comprises four companies backed up by an air detachment. ❒

US Special Forces insignia and qualification badges. From top to bottom and from left to right: 5th and 7th SF Groups badges, SOCOM metal badge (the SF's 'mother' unit); 1943-46 OSS-SOE 'wings'; rank and file SF cap badge; 12th and 20th SFG badges.
Centre: 10th and 11th SFG flashes; 1st Special Force cloth badge; 1956-62 10th SGF cloth badge.
Bottom: SF collar badge, 1st Special Operations Command cloth badge (subdued version); 18th SFG and SOCOM flashes.

DELTA FORCE

US Army Colonel Charles Beckwith trained with the British SAS for a year (1962-63) and, on his return home, sought to add a similar formation to US forces. After numerous attempts, the new force - 1st Special Forces Operational Detachment-Delta (or Delta for short) - was created on 19 November 1977. Its prime task was to deal with terrorists threatening American interests.

The escalation of terrorism was then a burning issue as demonstrated by the August 1972 Munich Olympic Games hostage incident (in which Israeli athletes were murdered), the 3/4 July 1976 Israeli raid on Entebbe to release hostages and the October 1977 Mogadishu rescue operation conducted by Germany's GSG 9.

The establishment of Delta Force was set at 1,200 men, organised like the SAS into 16 companies subdivided into 4-man teams but, fearing that they would lose their best men, other elite units such as the Special Forces and the Rangers did what they could to hinder recruiting. Their efforts however didn't prevent Beckwith from selecting 53 men out of an original 185 volunteers and by early 1979 the group amounted to 79 men and had expanded to 99 by autumn. Within 12 months, Delta Force had become so proficient that it could handle any type of anti-terrorist assignment.

The first real opportunity to display its skills cropped up in 1979 with Operation 'Eagle Claw': Iranian 'students' had broken into the US Embassy in Tehran and taken all the 53 staff members hostage. Tasked with this important and complex rescue mission, Delta Force soldiers and US Rangers were flown into Iran and delivered in a secluded area some 500km south-east of Tehran. From there, US Navy helicopters would fly them on to the embassy for the rescue. Things went according to plan until a helicopter collided on the ground with a C-130 after refuelling, killing five USAF crewmen and three marines. The decision was then made to cancel the operation.

This failure notwithstanding, Delta Force continued honing its skills, and throughout the 1980s, was deployed whenever aircraft were hijacked - although they never actually intervened. The unit comprises two squadrons subdivided into 16-man sections. Delta Force operates within CTJFF (Counter-Terrorist Joint Task Force), itself answering to NCA (National Command Authority). Screening tests are thorough and aimed at eliminating temperamental and individualistic candidates. This is then followed by a merciless selection at Fort Bragg (where candidates are airborne trained), Uwharrie in North Carolina and Camp Dawson in Virginia.

Training is practically identical to that of SAS. The 'happy few' (only about 20% of original applicants are retained) take up the 17-week basic training and most obtain the HALO and HAHO qualifications. Tuition also includes combat diving with closed-circuit aqualung. The training facilities at Fort Bragg are huge and include the famous Close Quarter Battle House better known as the 'Haunted House' and a Boeing 727 aircraft used to practise hostage rescue assaults. ❏

A Delta Force member, seen in April 1980 on Masirah Island in the Hormuz Straits, during Operation 'Eagle Claw'. The agents had gathered at this isolated spot to finalize the finer points of their mission - rescuing the hostages held in the US Tehran Embassy. The men were clad in a mixture of military and civilian garb as shown here: woollen knitwear and ordinary trousers with M-65 jacket and ALICE webbing. The commando is armed with an M-60 7.62mm machine-gun. Most Delta Force members taking part in 'Eagle Claw' were issued wth night vision equipment.

Delta Force qualification badges and insignia. Left: the unit's unofficial badge. Right, from top to bottom: the latest US Special Forces 'wings' (master, advanced and basic).

141

Special Forces (Green Berets) and 82nd
Airborne Paras during Operation 'Bright
Star' manoeuvres in Egypt.

SALVADOREAN PARA

The history of Salvadorean paras started in 1963 when six officers and 11 soldiers and NCOs trained at the Fort Benning Parachute School in the USA. On their return, a training center was set up on Llopango Air Base in the east of the country and the first course initiated in late 1963. In May 1964, the first airborne company was formed and included one command, three combat and one heavy weapons platoon. The first jumps (automatic) were made in 1966, and three years later a free-faller course was introduced. In 1973, US Green Berets of 7th SFG trained a parachute packer unit. In 1974 the company was expanded into a battalion, placed under army control in 1983, and later deployed as elite light infantry.

In 1972, 1st and 2nd *Grupos Operacions Especiales* were raised to combat guerillas. Trained by US Special Forces at the San Francisco Gotera Special Forces School, these units' missions were highly classified.

In 1979, the Americans poured in massive military aid to help El Salvador cope with escalating guerilla activities. Now enmeshed in total war, the Salvadorean Army created light intervention battalions (numbering less than 1,000 men each) to combat the different factions of FMNLF (Farabundo Marti National Liberation Front). In those days, the para battalions included 60% career soldiers and 40% volunteers. After selection and basic training, candidates obtained their 'wings' following five daytime and one night jump (using US T-10 and MC-1 parachutes). However, since the training cadre found itself more and more heavily committed in anti-guerilla warfare, airborne training was shortened and in 1979, the number of qualifying jumps was cut down to five. Since 1980 only one course has been run annually, instead of four to eight in the previous years. (The duration of basic training has been reduced to four weeks).

In time of war, the elite the *Para-caidistas* would not be assigned to a specific combat zone but deployed in the same way as a rapid intervention force. ·   ❑

Salvadorean airborne qualification badges. From left to right and from top to bottom: basic 'wings'; master badge (awarded for 65 jumps); senior badge (35 jumps) reserve airborne unit badge.

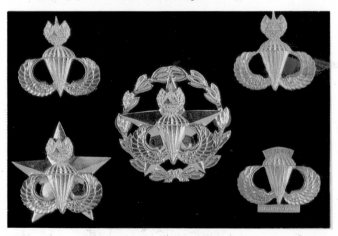

A para of Salvadorean Groupo de Operaciones Especiales in 1987. Unusually, the man wears the battalion patch above the Operaciones Especiales shoulder title. Wearing the camouflage outfit on exclusive issue to special forces, the man is entirely kitted out with American equipment (webbing, rucksack and grenades). He is armed with a XM-177 5.56mm assault rifle, well suited for jungle combat.

GUATEMALAN PARA

In 1942, two Guatemalta Air Force pilots returned from the United States and decided to form an airborne unit. After obtaining approval from their command, the two forerunners purchased American equipment and set up that same year a first 12-man airborne platoon.

However, this initiative petered out in the 50s. In 1960, under the spur of two superior officers, one qualified at Fort Benning and the other in Pau, the airborne forces were recreated in Guatemala. Originally 60 volunteers (officers and rank and file troopers) were sent to the United States for training. After qualifying, they returned to Guatemala and in January 1961 formed the training cadre of the newly-created Retalhuley parachute school. They were assisted by American instructors detached from Fort Benning. In June the first platoon was ready.

Two years later, the platoon became the 1st Compania de Paracaidistas de Fusilero. In 1966, the Compania de Fuerza Special was formed under the guidance of American Special Forces advisors. In spring 1970, the 2nd parachute company was created.

Six months later, the airborne forces were revamped and the 1st Battalon de Paracaidistas del Ejercito was commissioned. It comprised two para companies and a special force company. All these units were quartered in San Jose, a Pacific Coast base occupied by American forces from 1939 to 1949.

The battalion was then involved in a relentless struggle against Cuban-backed guerillas. It was so succesful in combating the insurgent groups, that since 1987, the guerillas have ceased all activities or surrendered in their hundreds when an amnesty was promised.

Currently, the Ejercito numbers 2,000 paras. All volunteers, they are subject to a careful selection and undergo two-months basic training followed by three-weeks airborne training. After six jumps (including one night jump), the trainees are allowed to wear the black beret with the red badge.

The transport fleet includes six C-47 aircraft and six Israeli Arava. The paras are armed with 5,56mm Galil assault rifles, FN MAG 58 machine guns, US 40mm M-79 grenade launchers and 60mm mortars. The main parachute is the US T-10 and the reserve chute the T-10A. Freefallers are issued with the MC-3 and Merlin Vector parachutes. Currently, the Guatemalan armed forces dispose of two airborne battalions: the 1st Battalion (1st Company 'Quetzales', 2nd Company 'Pentagones' and 3rd Company 'Flechas') and the 2nd Battalion (1st Company 'Cobras', 2nd Company 'Relampagos', 3rd Company 'Tecun' and 4th Company 'Olmecos'). ❐

Above left::
Guatemalan para corporal, member of the 1st Airborne Battalion, 2nd Company 'Pentagones', pictured in the San Marco province, Guatemala, in the summer of 1990. Over his woodland camouflage outfit, the sharpshooter wears an overall made of netting interwoven with pieces of canvas and strips of cloth. Remarkably efficient, this overall has its drawback to be very hot, especially in stifling jungle conditions. He is armed with a US 7,62mm M-21 sniping rifle fitted with a ART Springfield telescopic sight. To locate his targets, he uses M-22 7x50 binoculars.

From top to bottom and from left to right:
**Various Guatemalan airborne forces badges.
Standard airborne beret insignia. Basic qualification badge.
'Senior' airborne badge. 'Master' airborne badge. Freefaller qualification badge. 'Senior' freefaller qualification badge.
'Master' freefaller qualification badge. Dispatcher badge.
'Senior' dispatcher badge.
'Master' dispatcher badge.**

VENEZUELAN PARA

The history of Venezuelan paras started on 17 November 1948 when a group of about 100 officers, NCOs and men successfully completed the course at Fort Benning, USA, the US Army's parachute school. Soon afterwards, an airborne training company was created and three years later, on 10 December 1952 (anniversary of the Venezuelan Air Force), the unit was converted into an airborne training detachment.

Within a few years, ths detachment became the crucible for a whole generation of paratroopers leading Venezuelan Command to convert the unit into the Leonardo Chirinos Airborne Battalion. The unit took up quarters on Boca del Rio Air Base and within a year, the paras were transferred to Palo Negro Air Base to form a second unit, the Para Gual y Espana Battalion.

Created in 1965 and based at Maracay, the air force-controlled Aragua Airborne Group was soon placed under ground forces command as paras were assigned from both the air and ground forces (most officers were ground forces personnel). As a concession to the new service however, the men were issued with air force uniforms.

In 1978, a reorganisation of the ground forces took place and the Antonio Nicolas Briceno Battalion, specialising in anti-guerilla warfare and known as Green Beret Unit, was attached to the Aragua Airborne Group to replace the recently-disbanded Gual y Espana Battalion. The Group also comprised a commando company, entirely made up of career soldiers and specialising in recce and anti-terrorist actions.

Currently, most Venezuelan paras are professionals, (two-year conscripts represent about 36% of total army establishment) and are commissioned with the airborne battalions after the stringent selection and strenuous training in the same way as in neighbouring Brazil and Columbia. Venezuela's relationships with the latter are tense as paras train in the border zone, patrolling alongside 'Boinas Verdes' (green berets) soldiers specialising in jungle anti-guerilla warfare.

In all, Venezuela fields 13 such battalions, patterned on US Rangers units and operating within a 'jungle' division. The Venezuelan Navy has two airborne commando companies tasked with clearing beaches before the landing of naval infantry battalions. ❑

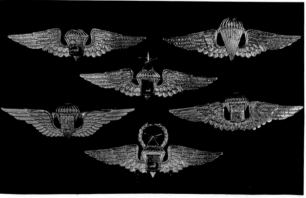

Various Venezuelan airborne qualification badges. From left to right and from top to bottom: basic airborne qualification badge (variant); basic qualification badge issued to personnel from outside the force; senior qualification badge, basic qualification badge (variant); jumpmaster badge with commando specialisation.

A corporal of the Aragua Airborne Group's Chirinos Battalion patrolling along the Columbian border in 1989. Clad in the standard all-service camouflage combat uniform, the para sports the airborne metal wings and the ubiquitous maroon beret worn by paras of all nations. Issued with equipment of US origin, the corporal is armed with an M-60 7.62mm light machine-gun, a weapon immortalised by the Vietnam War which, in spite of its reputation for unreliability, still provides effective fire support.

BRAZILIAN PARA

World War 2 was hardly over when, in December 1944, the Brazilian government decided to send 35 officers and NCOs to the Fort Benning Parachute School in Georgia, USA. Led by Captain de Pessoa, for several months the Brazilians practised parachuting and later established their own facilities to train the future airborne brigade. One year later, on 26 december 1945, a legal decree defining the creation of the Brazilian Airborne School was passed with the cadre being provided by the US-trained paras. Initially activated in Rio de Janeiro, the school was later transferred to Colina Longa and, in 1949, training of Brazilian paras started with the force expanding into an airborne unit. Two years later, the unit was designated Airborne Division and some of its components were decentralized, with the Santos Dumont Airborne Battalion's support company being based at Arroio dos Afonsos, while the artillery group (which later became 6th Airborne Field Artillery Group) was transferred to Deodoro.

In 1957, as US Green Berets started training Brazilian Special forces, the navy created an amphibious recce company to supplement its marine force. The men of this elite unit are trained like American SEALs and have obtained the airborne, Ranger and combat diver qualifications. When the Brazilian Army was reshuffled in 1968, the Airborne Brigade was transformed into the Parachute Brigade and has been officially designated as such since 1971. The formation comprises the 25th, 26th and 27th Airborne Infantry Battalions, the 8th Airborne Artillery group, the 1st Airborne Engineer Company, the 20th Airborne Support Battalion, a command and support company, a signals company, a pathfinder freefaller unit and a Special Forces detachment.

The Brigade also fields a dog-handling platoon trained for both rescue and combat duties. Almost exclusively made up of volunteers, Brazil's paras can be regarded as this country's shock troops and contribute to peacetime humanitarian and medical missions throughout the far-flung areas of their huge country.

Seen in 1987 near Rio de Janeiro, a Brazilian para of the Parachute Brigade's free-faller detachment. He wears the old camouflage fatigues pending the introduction of a new design (currently being distributed to the army's special forces and to the cadre of the famous Manaus jungle training centre). His webbing and magazine pouches are a mixture of Italian, American and locally-made equipment. Prominent on his fatigues are the shoulder patch and the cloth airborne qualification badge. He is armed with an unusual weapon, a sound-suppressed 9mm Beretta 14 submachine-gun (550 rounds/min, weighing 3kg). The barrel has been modified and the weapon is fitted with a laser scope. In this configuration, the submachine-gun can stealthily eliminate all kinds of opposition.

Various Brazilian airborne qualification badges and insignia. From left to right and from top to bottom. Instructor metal badge; cap metal badge; basic airborne badge; pathfinder free-faller qualification badge; Airborne Brigade patch, jumpmaster badge; marine commando badge; marine commando instructor badge.

CHILEAN SPECIAL FORCES

Aware that the topography of their country and its magnitude (4000km long for a width of about 200km) placed certain areas out of immediate reach, in the early 1960s the Chilean military decided to supplement its armed forces with airborne commandos. Despite being well aware that the creation of such a force capable of intervening anywhere on Chilean territory was urgent, several years elapsed before the 1st Battalion of Airborne Forces was raised on 2 April 1968. Similarly the Chilean Airborne and Special Forces School was activated on the same date at Peldehue near Santiago and placed under air force command.

The first course was initiated on 20 August of that year and was attended by a group of eight officers and five soldiers who were first led by the Battalion commander and then by the school commandant, Captain Iturriaga. After completing the course, the future instructors were sent to the US Special Forces (8th SF Group) jungle school in Panama to further their training.

After returning to Chile, the newly-formed cadre organised the first courses after slightly updating the curriculum. Four weeks were necessary to obtain the basic qualification after completing the training programme which included four daytime jumps and one at night (only instructors could apply for the free-faller qualification.)

Within two years, the Battalion was set up and tasked among other duties with the training of commandos. Until 1967 courses used to be provided by the Chilean Army Infantry School but it was decided to integrate airborne training with the commando programme and transfer it to the Special Forces School.

In addition to the para battalion, a special forces unit was created and modelled on the American example. As in all special forces, Chilean applicants are recruited after stringent selection. This eliminates about 80% of candidates who first train in Panama, then at Fort Benning, and later again in Latin America (Argentina and Brazil). Operating as a squadron answering directly to High Command, Chilean Special Forces played a major part when Allende's regime was overthrown by General Pinochet in 1973. The Special Forces were also engaged in the Andes alongside the 1st Army's Mountain Division where they successfully hounded down communist guerillas.

To be on an equal footing with ground forces, the Chilean navy has also just set up a combat diver team. Trained by American Seals, these divers are based at Vina del Mar and Valparaiso.

Currently, Chilean paras and commandos constitute the elite of their army, which is regarded by many as the best trained on the South American continent. ❒

Chilean airborne qualification badges. From top to bottom: current airborne badge issued to ground forces personnel; higher airborne badge; jumpmaster badge. Left: early airborne qualification badge with enamelled background issued in the 1960s. Right: different version with red background (a black version also exists) and smaller parachute.

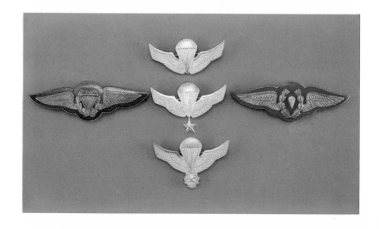

1988: a corporal of Chile's Special Forces Squadron pictured in the suburbs of the capital city, Santiago, during an anti-terrorist excercise. The man is shown in the latest camouflage outfit issued only to Special Forces, he wears a cap comforter and has smeared his hands and face with cam cream. The airborne qualification badge can be seen on his chest, while a combat knife, a grenade, and two four-magazine pouches are fastened to the webbing. The weapon is a sound-suppressed Model 11 Ingram 11.43mm submachine-gun.

ARGENTINE COMMANDO

The Argentine Special Forces were created in the 1960s with each of the three army services being allocated one or more elite units. The ground forces set up two groups of Special Forces; the navy its own seaborne commando group; and more recently, the air force created its own shock unit, the GOE.

The Argentines obtained American assistance and had their army and air force commando units trained by US Special Forces (In return, Washington requested that the Argentines trained Nicaragua's Contras.) The Argentines completed their training with courses at Fort Bragg in the USA. Interestingly, the seaborne commandos of Agrupacion de Comandos Amphibious were coached by British SAS instructors and were pitted against them a few years later in the Falklands War.

The ground forces field two commandos (601st and 602nd), modelled on US Rangers and composed exclusively of volunteers. Lasting three days, the selection of would-be commandos is very stringent and precedes the three-month course conducted at the Campo de Mayo Infantry School. There, trainees are coached in close-combat, jungle and urban fighting, and undergo navigation and survival courses. The commandos from the three services are parachute-qualified, have obtained their 'wings' from the Catamarca Airborne School and took part in the 1982 Falklands campaign. Answering to the air force, GOE is exclusively composed of free-fallers specialising in deep recce.

Operating within similar lines to the French 'Marine Commandos', the Buzo Tacticos won fame for their successful intervention in the 1982 Falklands War. On 2 April at dawn, 120 Buzo Tacticos landed and secured the islands.

The seaborne commandos belong to the active forces, are volunteers and trained to operate on land, sea and air.

They are all parachute qualified, and have attended the combat diver and sabotage courses. Before the Falklands War, Argentine commandos often took part in joint training programmes with US SEALs and the British SBS. ❒

Below. **Several badges on current or past issue to Argentinian commandos.** *From top to bottom and from left to right:* **the current airborne qualification badge; the gilded model for officers (also issued to navy and ground forces personnel since 1952); the seaborne commando badge; the army commando cloth badge; the early airborne qualification badge issued to air force personnel (gilded for officers and bronze for rank and file). Two variants of the airborne qualification badge issued to air force personnel (the gilded model is the officer variant)**

Above.
Pictured in April 1992 in the Falklands, a member of Argentina's 601st Army Commando in camouflage fatigues reminiscent of the American pattern. Field dressings are taped to his helmet. Like all Argentine forces in the Falklands, the commando has ben issued with plastic goggles to cope with the glare which often prevails in the southern hemisphere. His assault rifle is a FAL/FAP, fitted with a bipod, and reputedly superior to the weapons used by British forces. On his webbing, he carries two Argentine-manufactured GME FMK2 MO hand grenades. The 601st landed in the Falklands on 24 April and was joined by the 602nd one month later. Together, the two units conducted deep forays into the hinterland to detect British landings.

149

MALVINAS

VOLVEREMOS

Several phases of the harsh training that Army commandos of Agentinian 601st and 602nd 'Compania de Comando' are put through before graduating.

151

AFRICA

MOROCCO

RHODESIA

SOUTH AFRICA

MOROCCAN PARA

Regarded as one of the most reliable armies in north Africa, Moroccan forces have always been renowned for their bravery. Shortly after gaining independence in 1956, Morocco emulated France by providing its forces with a sizeable airborne spearhead. As their relationship with Paris were at a particularly low ebb, Rabat turned to the United States for assistance and Washington was only too delighted to provide several dozens of advisors to train Moroccan paras, airmen and tank crews.

Morroco's 1st Airborne Infantry Brigade was fully operational by the end of the 1960s and blooded soon afterwards in 1963 when it came up against Algerian forces in the Tindouf area. Moroccan paras were also deployed in a more peaceful context by contributing a contingent to UN Blue Helmets in the Congo when that colony was in the throes of independence.

In 1967 and 1973, Morocco was involved in the Arab-Israeli wars and in November 1973, Moroccan paras were pitted against their Israeli counterparts in the bitter fighting for Mount Hermon in Syria.

Employed in the rapid intervention role, two para battalions were dispatched in 1976 to the Spanish Sahara and fought anti-partition Mauritanian troops. Rabat's paras were later involved in anti-guerilla action against Polisario insurgents, a war which has continued unabated to the present day. In April 1977, three para battalions were sent to Zaire to help that country repel incursions by Katangan rebels. One year later, the Moroccans were dispatched again to Zaire where they stayed for more than a year after French para-legionnaires had intervened decisively in Shaba and Kolwezi.

Distributed into one command and services and five combat battalions, the 1st Airborne Brigade totals 5,000 men and has its own training facilities. In addition, Moroccan Royal Armed Forces field three commando battalions based at Rabat-Sale and led by Colonel Sour Allah. Composed of about 50% conscripts, the Brigade is kept as a general reserve unit. The command and services battalion, two combat battalions and the training unit are quartered at Rabat Sale while one combat battalion is deployed at Shkirat and two others are deployed in the south and guard the 'wall', a defence line built to counter incursions by Polisario insurgents (these two units answer directly to the King). Moroccan airborne units only have light armament: 106mm recoilless guns, 120mm mortars, 14.50mm twin guns, and Milan, TOW and HOT missile launchers.

Benefiting from its improved relationship with France in the 1960s, Rabat obtained military assistance and currently, more than 100 French advisors are on duty with Moroccan training units (with the exception of Kenitra where the cadre consists of US Special Forces instructors). Since 1985, numerous Morrocan para officers and NCOs have been sent to the Arab Emirates on rotation (5,000 Moroccan soldiers were deployed in the Gulf). Several commando officers are attached to forces in Gabon while in Guinea, 360 paras provide President Mbasogo's presidential guard .

Although ceasefire agreements have been signed recently, the war against Polisario is still smouldering and gives Morrocan paras the opportunity to acquire first hand combat experience. ❐

1987: a Moroccan para of 3rd Battalion, 1 Airborne Infantry Brigade, during a mission on the southern front. Belonging to a deep recce unit (issued with jeeps for raids against the Polisario), the man is clad in a French-inspired 'lizard' camouflage combat uniform and kitted out with a mixture of French and American equipment. Strapped to his forehead is a US AN/PVS-5A light intensifyer used for night combat. He is armed with a French-made AA-52 MG, an obsolescent but still efficient weapon, shown here in its light machine-gun configuration. The green beret, common to ground forces, is rolled up and tucked under the shoulder strap.

Representative Moroccan airborne badges. From top to bottom and from left to right: early airborne qualification badge (introduced in the 1960s); instructor badge; airborne qualification badge (second series); variant of the previous model; airborne badge (third series); instructor badge variant; para-commando badge.

RHODESIAN SELOUS SCOUT

Between their commissioning in December 1973 to their disbandment in March 1980, Rhodesian Selous Scouts performed so well that they are still regarded as the best bush combat unit ever deployed on the African continent. Spearhead of the Rhodesian forces, Selous Scouts have accounted for more terrorists killed than all the other army units together!

Since independence in 1965, Rhodesia became increasingly concerned about the growing terrorist threat. Consequently in 1973 Rhodesia developed its armed forces and raised the unique Tracker Combat Unit which was given the name of Fredrick Selous, one of her most famous explorers. The Selous Scouts' brief was simple: to eliminate ZANLA and ZIPRA terrorists in Rhodesia, Mozambique, Zambia and Botswana by clandestine means. Unlike the Rhodesian SAS, the Selous Souts' activities were unrestricted and they could engage the enemy at will. Professionalism was the key to the Scout's success and their figures speak for themselves: the Scouts accounted for 70% of all insurgents killed by Rhodesian forces, for the loss of only 40 of their men.

During the war years, the establishment of the force never amounted to more than 1,500 men, trained and led by the famous Colonel Reid-Deily, a former SAS member who had served in Malaysia. The members of this racially mixed force (natives made up 80% of some units) were volunteers, handpicked after a merciless selection that eliminated all but 15% of applicants. Training revolved broadly around tracking and survival, and in addition, all Scouts were airborne qualified (the force included free-fallers).

The Scouts' basic unit was the 'troop', subdivided into three eight-man squads. Each squad was distributed into two teams which, because of their small size, could operate undetected. In addition to deep recce, the Scouts carried out numerous clandestine missions in guerilla-held areas to gather intelligence and eliminate leaders (native African Scouts were particularly well suited to these tasks).

The unit took part in Rhodesian raids against 'terro' units and distinguished itself in the 1976 operation against the Nyadzonya camp in Mozambique. In this action, less than 100 Scouts surrounded more than 5,000 guerillas, accounting for at least 600 of them. Reportedly, Selous Scouts often posed as Soviet or East German advisors better to infiltrate ZANLA or ZIPRA guerilla units. Although free to choose their own armament, Selous Scouts often used Soviet-made AK-47s, RPK and RPD light machine-guns. When a native Rhodesian leader was elected in 1980, the Scouts were quietly disbanded and many joined the ranks of the South African army to fight against ANC and SWAPO terrorists. ❏

1977: a Selous Scout in Rhodesia. As often with elite forces Selous Scouts could choose their fighting gear and were often seen operating in T-shirts and shorts. (East German or even FRELIMO uniforms were also worn.) In the picture, the man wears a Rhodesian camouflage combat jacket, with shortened trousers and tennis shoes - ideal for stalking guerillas in the bush. His British 58 Pattern webbing has been modified to accommodate non-regulation magazines for his camouflaged FAL assault rifle. Originally issued with FALs, the Scouts made increasingly frequent use of sturdier Soviet-made AK-47 and RPDs (captured ammunition was always available in vast quantities). Trained like the British SAS, the Selous Scouts were also proficient in survival and tracking techniques.

Selous Scout badges and insignia. From top to bottom and from left to right: Selous Scout airborne qualification badge; silver collar badge; airborne patch; cap badge; embroidered shoulder patch adorned with a lion and worn on the right sleeve of fatigues and parade dress.

SOUTH AFRICAN KOEVOET

In South West Africa, the first anti-guerilla operations took place in 1966 and were carried out by the anti-terrorists units of the South African police.

Headquartered at Windhook, these units retained the same organisation until 1989, but changed their name in 1980 to become known as SWAP (South West African Police) instead of SAP (South African Police).

In 1979, SAP's Security Branch created the Koevoet (Operation K), an anti-terrorist unit modelled on the Rhodesian Selous Scouts, with 10 South African and 64 members of the local police. The Koevoet had mission to roam the bush and gather intelligence on behalf of the Army intervention units.

But the results were not up to the expectations of the Security Branch, and South African command decided to give the Koevoet the means they needed to make the most of their informations. Soon, the unit was issued with armoured vehicles and in less than three months, had successfully fought it out with terrorists in 36 engagements.

'Operation K' was soon enlarged to include three units based in Kavango, Ovamboland and Kaokoland. The headquarters was established at Oshakati, and after addition of an intelligence team, the Koevoet were reorganised into combat groups and carried out secret missions in Angola.

Led by an officer or NCO from the Security Branch, each combat group fielded 40 to 50 soldiers, equipped with four Casspir APCs and a supply truck.

The men were recruited in Ovamboland, and included former rebels. The groups were deployed during major operations but acted on their own most of the time.

In each combat group each man contributed his knowledge of the terrain, personal skill and initiative to the success of Koevoet. During the engagements, the men often had the advantageof fighting from their vehicles, which gave them a good vision of the battlefield and excellent mobility.

In this type of warfare, SWAPO terrorists never fought on equal terms, and before independence, their attacks were often suicidal. The Koevoet were disbanded when the South African army left Namibia.

Opposite Left
Depicted in 1988 at the Koevoet HQ in Oshakati, this South African officer wears the South African Police camouflaged combat outfit and a lightweight, recce-commando chest webbing holding more magazines than the normal issue vest. He is armed with an AK-47. On operations, each group leader acted as radio operator and was issued with a receiver transmitter set.

Opposite, right:
Various badges of Koevoet units operating in Namibia (South-east Africa). Each group had its own insignia and sported it on the shoulder or on a T-shirt indicating the unit's location. Centre, left and right: Koevoet tracker unit patches.
(Badges supplied by Christopher Lee)

156

SOUTH AFRICAN RECCE COMMANDO

A very secret force, South African Recce Commandos compare well man for man with British and Australian SAS and undoubtly rank among the world's finest special units.

In the 1970s, when the communist-inspired African National Congress began to raise threats at home and on its borders, South African command raised an experimental airborne unit and had it trained for special missions into enemy territory. The experiment was successful and led to the creation of 1st Reconnaissance Commando. Commanded by the famous Colonel Jan Breytenbach, the battalion-sized unit was exclusively composed of 44th Airborne Brigade 'Parabats'.

The South Africans felt even more insecure when the Portuguese pulled out of neighbouring Angola and conducted operations deep into that country to the outskirts of its capital city, Luanda. During these operations the Recce Commandos' were used as conventional ground forces. In July 1978, 4th Recce Commando was transferred to Langebaan for amphibious training.

Raised six months later, 5th Recce was exclusively staffed with natives as this unit was meant for incursions into bordering countries (Angola, Bostwana, Rhodesia, Mozambique and Zambia). In 1980, numerous Rhodesian SAS and Selous Scouts found their way to South Africa when their war ended and formed the cadre of 3rd and 6th Recce Commandos - although both units were disbanded one year later.

Recce Commandos had by now become bush combat specialists and until 1988 (or so official records would have us believe) were involved in all major sweeps against SWAPO, ANC and Angolan FAPLA insurgents.

When defining the admission criteria for Recce applicants, the South Africans evolved what is regarded as the hardest screening process of all. Spread over 42 weeks, the selection/training procedure is so stringent that the success rate is hardly 10%! Most candidates originate from the 'bush' and are, on average, 19 years of age; although the cadre still includes former Rhodesian SAS and Selous Scouts. Airborne and amphibious training is compulsory and all commandos familiarise themselves with the rigours of the desert - especially the chilly nights - during a survival course in the Drakensberg Range. The graduation tests involves a 110km trek through the barren Phalaborwa region (near the Kruger National Reserve), covered in three days and interspersed with obstacles and proficiency checks.

Up till now, only 2,000 Recce Commandos have made it through since the unit was officially commissioned in 1972 and of that number, about 700 are currently on active service. Four Recce Commandos and a reserve unit are on strength with the South African armed forces and operate within the 1st Special Forces Brigade. The Recce Commando units are based at Durban, Langebaan, Pretoria and Phalaborwa. ❑

Recce Commando badges and insignia. From top to bottom and from left to right: 1st Recce Commando badge; Jaric (Joint Air/Recce/Intelligence) 'wings'; basic airborne qualification badge. Bottom row: instructor badge; 1st Recce Commando chest badge; 4th Recce Commando chest badge; 1st Recce Commando Brigade badge.

A lance corporal of 1st Recce Commando in February 1988 during a mission on Angola's southern border. The platoon's radio operator, he wears a tan outfit with good camouflage properties for bush conditions. His transceiver is fitted with a throat microphone for maximum discretion during transmissions. He is armed with a 5.56mm R-4, the locally-made version of the Israeli Galil. The chest webbing has been designed for protracted use.

157

ACKNOWLEDGEMENTS

The author wishes to thank all the specialists and collectors who kindly supplied photographs to illustrate this book.

PHOTO CREDITS

Eric MICHELETTI : 4, 5, 14, 18, 42, 56, 92, 116, 130, 134, 138, 139, 142, 143.

Yves DEBAY : 8, 10, 12, 20, 21, 22, 26, 27, 30, 34, 38, 40, 44, 46, 48, 54, 62, 68, 70, 72, 74, 76, 82, 84, 88, 118, 120, 122, 123, 132, 133, 136, 138, 139, 158.

Jean-Pierre HUSSON : 16, 52, 58, 60.

Gilles RIVET : 50, 150, 151.

Karie HAMILTON : 126.

Anthony ROGERS : 112.

Peter RUSSEL : 24.

Robin ADSHEAD : 28.

US NAVY : 124.

Private collections : 78, 108.

Design: Stéphane BALLE, Jean-Marie MONGIN, Patrick LESIEUR. © PLST
UK Co-ordinator: Alexandra GARDINER

ISBN : 2 908 182 25 4
Publisher' s number : 2-908182.
Published by **Histoire & Collections**
19, avenue de la République. 75011 Paris, France.
Tél. : International *(1) 40.21.18.20*
Fax : International *(1) 40.21.97.55*

Editorial composition : *Macintosh II FX, X Press* and Adobe *Illustrator*

Photography *: SCIPE,* Paris.

Colour separation *: Ozaland,* Paris.

Printed by *SIB,* Saint-Léonard, France, on 31 August 1993

ISBN: **2 908 182 25 4**
HISTOIRE & COLLECTIONS
P.O. Box 327, Poole, Dorset BH15 2 RG, UK

1442